# CAMBRIDGE LIBRARY COLLECTION

*Books of enduring scholarly value*

## Literary Studies

This series provides a high-quality selection of early printings of literary works, textual editions, anthologies and literary criticism which are of lasting scholarly interest. Ranging from Old English to Shakespeare to early twentieth-century work from around the world, these books offer a valuable resource for scholars in reception history, textual editing, and literary studies.

## Thomas Carlyle

Moncure Daniel Conway (1832–1907), the son of a Virginian plantation-owner, became a Unitarian minister but his anti-slavery views made him controversial. He later became a freethinker, and following the outbreak of the Civil War, which deeply divided his own family, he left the United States for England in 1863. He gained a reputation as the 'least orthodox preacher in London', and was acquainted with many figures in the literary and scientific world, including Charles Dickens and Charles Darwin. This memoir of Thomas Carlyle, another friend, was published in 1881 soon after Carlyle's death. Carlyle had not wanted to be the subject of a biography, and reluctantly authorised J. A. Froude to write one, but Conway rushed into print this somewhat hagiographical account because he was concerned, with reason, about the damage Froude's frank biography (published in 1882–4 and also reissued in this series) might do to Carlyle's reputation.

T0381670

Cambridge University Press has long been a pioneer in the reissuing of out-of-print titles from its own backlist, producing digital reprints of books that are still sought after by scholars and students but could not be reprinted economically using traditional technology. The Cambridge Library Collection extends this activity to a wider range of books which are still of importance to researchers and professionals, either for the source material they contain, or as landmarks in the history of their academic discipline.

Drawing from the world-renowned collections in the Cambridge University Library and other partner libraries, and guided by the advice of experts in each subject area, Cambridge University Press is using state-of-the-art scanning machines in its own Printing House to capture the content of each book selected for inclusion. The files are processed to give a consistently clear, crisp image, and the books finished to the high quality standard for which the Press is recognised around the world. The latest print-on-demand technology ensures that the books will remain available indefinitely, and that orders for single or multiple copies can quickly be supplied.

The Cambridge Library Collection brings back to life books of enduring scholarly value (including out-of-copyright works originally issued by other publishers) across a wide range of disciplines in the humanities and social sciences and in science and technology.

# Thomas Carlyle

MONCURE DANIEL CONWAY

CAMBRIDGE
UNIVERSITY PRESS

CAMBRIDGE UNIVERSITY PRESS

Cambridge, New York, Melbourne, Madrid, Cape Town,
Singapore, São Paolo, Delhi, Mexico City

Published in the United States of America by Cambridge University Press, New York

www.cambridge.org
Information on this title: www.cambridge.org/9781108045346

© in this compilation Cambridge University Press 2012

This edition first published 1881
This digitally printed version 2012

ISBN 978-1-108-04534-6 Paperback

THOMAS CARLYLE.

*From a Photograph by Elliott & Fry.*

# THOMAS CARLYLE

BY

MONCURE D. CONWAY

*ILLUSTRATED*

NEW YORK

HARPER & BROTHERS, FRANKLIN SQUARE

1881

# PREFACE.

EARLY in the year 1863, when I first visited England, Emerson gave me a letter of introduction to Thomas Carlyle, which at once secured for me a gracious reception and kindly entertainment from the author and his wife at Chelsea. It was their custom to receive their friends in the evening, and I was invited to join their circle as often as it might be convenient to me. As time went on, this evening circle at Carlyle's became smaller, and many a time I was the only guest present. I was also invited by Carlyle to share his walks, after he had given up the horseback exercise he used to take. These afternoon walks were long, generally through Kensington Gardens, Hyde Park, and even into Piccadilly. I was careful never to interrupt his hours of literary labor, and always to obey Mrs. Carlyle's kindly intimations as to his habits and exigencies. My relations with the memorable home at Chelsea were always, and to the last, very pleasant, never marred by any incident or word to be thought of now with regret.

This little book which I now send out to the world was veritably written by Carlyle himself. However inadequately transcribed and conveyed, these pages do faithfully follow impressions made by his own word and spirit upon my mind during an intercourse of many years. Nothing has been imported into them from other publications which have appeared since his death. The letters of Carlyle, and that charming one written by Emerson just after his first visit to him which is added to them, have been in-trusted to me by my friend Alexander Ireland—au-thor of an excellent bibliographical work on the writings of Hazlitt, Lamb, and Leigh Hunt — the valued friend of both Carlyle and Emerson. The suppressions indicated in those letters are of matters properly private — as, indeed, are various withheld notes of my own—and not things omitted with any theoretical purpose.

I have written out my notes and my memories with the man still vividly before me, and, as it were, still speaking; and, I must venture to add, it is a man I can by no means identify with any image that can be built up out of his "Reminiscences." I do not wish to idealize Carlyle, but cannot admit that the outcries of a broken heart should be accepted as the man's true voice, or that measurements of men and memories as seen through burning tears should be recorded as characteristic of his heart or judgment. This sketch of mine is written and published in loyalty to the memory of those two at Chelsea whom, amid whatever differences of conviction, I honored and loved.

# LIST OF ILLUSTRATIONS.

# Part I.
# THOMAS CARLYLE

# THOMAS CARLYLE.

## I.

THE real record of Carlyle's life will be a long task, employing not only many human hands, but even the hand of Time itself.

While writing his "History of Friedrich II.," Carlyle had prepared—as, indeed, the growth of the work had demanded—a special study at the top of his house in Chelsea, in which only that paper, book, or picture was admitted which was in some way connected with the subject in hand. One side of the room was covered from floor to ceiling with books; two others were adorned with pictures of persons or battles; and through these books and pictures was distributed the man he was trying to put together in comprehensible shape. But even more widely was Carlyle himself distributed. In what part of the earth have not his lines gone out and his labors extended? On how many hearts and minds, on how many lives, has he engraved passages which are transcripts of his own life, without which it can never be fully told? To report this one life, precious contributions must be brought from the lives of Goethe, Emerson, Jeffrey, Brewster, Sterling, Leigh Hunt, Mill, Mazzini, Margaret Fuller, Harriet Martineau, Faraday. But how go on with the long catalogue? At its end, could that be reached, there would remain the equally important memories of lives less known, from which in the future may come incidents casting fresh light upon this central figure of two generations; and, were all told, time alone can bring the perspective through which his genius and character can be estimated. In one sense, Carlyle was as a city set upon a hill, that cannot be hid; in another, he was an "open secret," hid by the very simplicity of his unconscious disguises, the frank perversities whose meaning could be known only by those close enough to hear the heart-beat beneath them; and many who have fancied that they had him rightly labelled with some moody utterance, or safely pigeon-holed in some outbreak of a soul acquainted with grief, will be found to have measured the oak by its mistletoe.

Those who have listened to the wonderful conversation of Carlyle know well its impressiveness and its charm: the sympathetic voice now softening to the very gentlest, tenderest tone as it searched far into some sad life, little known or regarded, or

perhaps evil spoken of, and found there traits
to be admired, or signs of nobleness,—then rising
through all melodies in rehearsing the deeds of heroes; anon breaking out with illumined thunders
against some special baseness or falsehood, till one
trembled before the Sinai smoke and flame, and
seemed to hear the tables break once more in his
heart: all these, accompanied by the mounting, fad-
ing fires in his cheek, the light of the eye, now serene as heaven's blue, now flashing with wrath, or
presently suffused with laughter, made the outer
symbols of a genius so unique that to me it had
been unimaginable had I not known its presence
and power. His conversation was a spell; when I
had listened and gone into the darkness, the enchant-
ment continued; sometimes I could not sleep till
the vivid thoughts and narratives were noted in
writing. It is mainly from these records of conver-
sations that the following pages are written out, with
addition of some other materials obtained by personal inquiries made in Scotland and in London. I
realized many years ago that my notes contained
matter that might some day be useful, especially to
my American countrymen, in forming a just estimate and judgment of one whose expressions were
often unwelcome; and this conviction has made me
increasingly careful, as the years went on, to remark
any variations of his views, and his responses to crit-

icisms made so frequently upon statements of his which had been resented. I do not in the least modify, nor shall I set forth these things in such order or relation as to illustrate any theory of my own. He who spoke his mind through life must so speak on, though he be dead.

## II.

Thomas Carlyle was born on the 4th of December, 1795, at Ecclefechan, Dumfriesshire. The small stone house still stands. It was a favorite saying of his that great men are not born among fools. "There was Robert Burns," he said one day; "I used often to hear from old people in Scotland of the good sense and wise conversation around that little fireside where Burns listened as a child. Notably there was a man named Murdoch who remembered all that; and I have the like impression about the early life of most of the notable men and women I have heard or read of. When a great soul rises up, it is generally in a place where there has been much hidden worth and intelligence at work for a long time. The vein runs on, as it were, beneath the surface for a generation or so, then bursts into the light in some man of genius, and oftenest that seems to be the end of it." Carlyle was thinking of other persons than himself, but there are few lives that could better point his thought. Nothing could

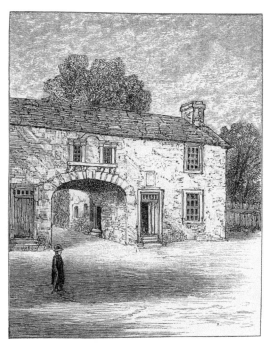

BIRTHPLACE OF THOMAS CARLYLE.

be more incongruous with the man and his life than
the attempt once made to get up a Carlyle "pedi-
gree."

But the vigor of the lowly stock was proved by
the strong individuality it steadily developed, and
in none more notably than the father of Thomas.
The humble stone-mason certainly "builded better
than he knew," though he lived long enough to hear
his son's name pronounced with honor throughout
the kingdom. An aged Scotch minister who knew
him well told me that old James Carlyle was "a
character." "Earnest, energetic, of quick intellect,
and in earlier life somewhat passionate and pugna-
cious, he was not just the man to be popular among
his rustic neighbors of Annandale; but they respect-
ed his pronounced individuality, felt his strong will,
and his terse, epigrammatic sayings were remembered and repeated many years after his death
(1832). In the later years of his life he became a
more decidedly religious character, and the natural
asperities of his character and manner were much
softened."

Mr. James Routledge, in an Indian periodical,
*Mookerjee's Magazine*, October, 1872, says:

"I was interested enough in Mr. Carlyle the
younger to make a special tour, some years ago, to
learn something of Mr. Carlyle the elder; and from
what I gathered the reader may be pleased with a

few scraps, as characteristic of the school of 'Sartor
Resartus.' Mr. Carlyle's landlord was one General
Sharpe, of whom little is now known, though he was
a great man in those days. On one occasion James
Carlyle and he had a quarrel, and James was heard
to say, in a voice of thunder, 'I tell thee what, Mat-
thew Sharpe'—a mode of salutation that doubtless
astonished General Sharpe; but it was 'old James
Carlyle's way,' and was not to be altered for any
General in existence. There was much in the old
man's manner of speaking that never failed to at-
tract attention. A gentleman resident in the local-
ity told me that he remembered meeting him one
very stormy day, and saying, 'Here's a fearful day,
James;' which drew forth the response, 'Man, it's a'
that; it's roaring doon our glen like the cannon o'
Quebec.' My informant added, 'I never could forget that sentence.' James had also a wondrous power of fixing upon characteristic names for all manner of persons, and nailing his names to the individuals for life. Samuel Johnson was 'Surly Sam,' and
so on—a gift which has come among us in a more
livable form from the pen of his son. Mr. Carlyle
was a stern Presbyterian—a Burgher; held no terms
with prelacy or any other ungodly offshoot from the
Woman of Babylon, but clung to the 'auld Buke,'
without note or comment, as his only guide to heav-
en. He was one of the elders of his church when

its pastor, having received a call from a church where his stipend would be better than that of Ecclefechan, applied for leave to remove. The church met, and lamentation was made for the irreparable loss. After much nonsense had been spoken, Mr. Carlyle's opinion was asked. 'Pay the hireling his wages and let him go,' said the old man; and it was done. Mr. Carlyle had a thorough contempt for any one who said, 'I can't.' 'Impossible' was not in his vocabulary. Once, during harvest-time, he was taken seriously ill. No going to the field, Mr. Carlyle, for weeks to come: water-gruel, doctor's bottles, visiting parson, special prayers — poor old James Carlyle! Pshaw! James was found crawling to the field early next morning, but still an idler among workers. He looked at the corn, provokingly ripe for the sickle; and then, stamping his foot fiercely to the ground, he said, 'I'll gar mysel' work at t' harvest.' And he did work at it like a man. On one occasion a reverend gentleman had been favoring the congregation of Mr. Carlyle's church with a terrible description of the last judgment. James listened to him calmly; but when the sermon was finished, he came out of his pew, and, placing himself before the reverend gentleman and all the congregation, he said, aloud, 'Ay, ye may thump and stare till yer een start frae their sockets, but you'll na gar me believe such stuff as that.'

" If the reader will now go back with me to those days, and view for a few minutes the little farm at Mainhill, after the fair, honest, and well-earned hours of evening rest have fully arrived, we shall, in all probability, find Mr. Carlyle reading from the Bible —not for fashion's sake, not to be seen and praised by men, but for reproof, for correction, for instruction in righteousness; and his children will be listening, as children should.   Refused his proper place in society for want of learning, we shall see this brave old man doing the next best thing to moulding the age—training his children to do that which he felt a power within him capable of performing, but for which the means—the mechanical means, the verb and pronoun kind of thing—were denied.   Such was the father, and such the earliest school of Thomas Carlyle."

Of the many anecdotes told of this elder Carlyle, one seems to be characteristic not only of the man, but of the outer environment amid which Thomas passed his earlier life.   On the occasion of a marriage of one of the sons, the younger members of the household proposed that a coat of paint should be given the house; but the old man resisted this scheme for covering the plain walls with the varnish of falsehood.   An attempt was made by the majority to set aside his will, but, unfortunately, old Mr. Carlyle was at home when the painters arrived, and planting himself in the doorway, demanded what they wanted. They replied that they "cam' tae pent the house." "Then," returned the old man, "ye can jist slent the bog wi' yer ash-baket feet, for ye'll pit nane o' yer glaur on ma door." The painters needed no translation of this remark, and "slent the bog"—i. e., went their ways. Paint to the sturdy old stone-mason meant simply so much slime; for it would appear that the Latin *clara* and French *glaire* are represented in Scotland by *clarts* and *glaur*—equiv-alents for mud, and more appropriately used for mud of a viscous character. I have sometimes thought that if the father had been able to admit those house-painters, the son's destiny might have been different. His dislike of rhyme and poetic measures, after showing that he could excel in the same, and all literary architecture, had in it an echo of that paternal horror of "glaur." He scented a falsehood from afar. Some one spoke of "England's *prestige.*" "Do you remember what prestige means?" asked he, sharply: "it is the Latin word for a lie."

As James Carlyle acquired more means he added to the small house in Ecclefechan a further building, which now stands behind the other in what is still called "Carlyle's Close." Afterwards he took to farming, and became the possessor of the neighbor-ing farm and homestead of over two hundred acres, called Scotsbrig. For some years previously he had

become more of an architect than a stone-mason.
The stone-mason's craft often furnished Carlyle
with his metaphors, and he always had a special
horror of architectural shams. Once as we were
walking together he remarked the flimsiness of some
house-walls just going up. "Every brick in them
is a lie. A necessary part, I suppose, of the superla-
tive ugliness of so many people crowding together.
The cities are all cabbaging out in this way. The
house I live in (at Chelsea) was built by honest men.
The brick and mortar have hardened together with
time, and made a wall which is one solid stone, and
it will stand there till Gabriel's trump blows it
down."

### III.

In order to introduce here, as well as my notes
and memory enable me, some of Carlyle's own ram-
bling reminiscences of those who were the presiding
destinies of his early life, it will be necessary to pass
to a comparatively recent period, and attend him to
an eminence in his life from which those young
years were beheld in natural perspective. And my
reader must pardon me for now and then turning
into a by-way on our road.

It was in the evening of the day when Carlyle was
inaugurated Lord Rector of Edinburgh University
that he himself told me most fully the story of his
early life, and of his struggles in that ancient city

which had now decorated itself in his honor. That day was the culmination of his personal history. No pen has yet described the events of that day, and the main fact of it, in their significance or picturesqueness. Nor can that be wondered at; the background against which they stood out were the weary trials, the long unwatched studies, the poverty and want, amid which the little boy of fourteen began to climb the rugged path which ended on this height. When on that bright day (the 2d of April, 1866) Carlyle entered the theatre in Edinburgh, the scene was one for which no memory of the old university could have prepared him. Beside him walked the venerable Sir David Brewster, fourteen years his senior, who first recognized his ability, and first gave him literary work to do. The one now Principal, the other Lord Rector, they walked forward in their gold-laced robes of office, while the professors, the students, the ladies, stood up, cheering, waving their hats, books, handkerchiefs, as if some wild ecstasy were sweeping over the assembly. Who were these around him? The old man sat and scanned for a little the faces before him. His eye alights on Huxley, and not far away is the face of his friend Tyndall, all sunshine. Another and another face from London, a score of aged faces that bring up memories from this and that quiet retreat of Scotland, and the occasion begins to weave its potent influences around the man who had never faced audience since, some twenty-six years before, he had celebrated "Heroes," and among them some less heroic than this new Lord Rector. On that last occasion, in the Edwards Street Institute, London, Carlyle brought a manuscript, and found it much in his way. On the next evening he brought some notes, but these also tripped him up, till he left them. The rest of the lectures were given without a note, simply like his conversation, and they required very little alteration when they came to be printed. For this Edinburgh occasion, also, Carlyle at first thought of writing something; he made out some headings and a few notes, and carried them in his pocket to the theatre, but he did not look at them.

What that address really was no one can imagine who has only read it. Throughout, it was phenomenal, like some spiritualized play of the elements. Ere he began, Carlyle, much to the amusement of the students, shook himself free of the gold-laced gown; but it was not many minutes before he had laid aside various other conventionalities: the grand sincerity, the drolleries, the auroral flashes of mystical intimation, the lightnings of scorn for things low and base—all of these severally taking on physiognomical expression in word, tone, movement of the head, color of the face, really seemed to bring before us a being whose physical form was purely a transparency of thought and feeling.

What a figure stood there before us! The form, stately though slender and somewhat bent, conveyed the impression of a powerful organization ; the head, well curved and long, moving but rarely from side to side, then slowly; the limbs, never fidgety, buttressing, like quaint architecture, the lofty head and front of the man: these characters at once made their impression. But presently other and more subtle characteristics came out on the face and form before us, those which time and fate, thought and experience, had added to the man which nature had given them. The rugged brow, softened by the silvered hair, had its inscriptions left by the long years of meditation and of spiritual sorrow; the delicate mouth, whose satire was sympathetic, never curling the lip nor sinking to sarcasm; the blond face, with its floating colors of sensibility, and the large luminous eye—these made the outer image of Carlyle as he stood and spake, when even the gray-haired were gathered at his feet, listening like children held by a tale of Wonderland.

When Carlyle sat down there was an audible sound, as of breath long held, by all present; then a cry from the students, an exultation; they rose up, all arose, waving their arms excitedly; some pressed forward, as if wishing to embrace him, or to clasp his knees; others were weeping: what had been heard that day was more than could be reported; it was the ineffable spirit that went forth from the deeps of a great heart and from the ages stored up in it, and deep answered unto deep.

When, after the address, Carlyle came out to the door, a stately carriage was waiting to take him to the house of Mr. Erskine, of Linlathen, but he begged to be allowed to walk. He had no notion, however, what that involved. No sooner did the delighted crowd, or friendly mob, discover that the Lord Rector was setting out to walk through the street than they extemporized a procession, and followed him, several hundred strong, with such clamorous glorification that he found it best to take a cab. As he did so, he turned and gave the rather ragged part of the crowd a steady, compassionate look, and said, softly, as if to himself, "Poor fellows! poor fellows!"

During the dinner that evening, at which Mr. Erskine entertained Lord Neaves, Dr. John Brown, and other Edinburgh celebrities, Carlyle was very happy, and conversed in the finest humor; he enlightened us, as I remember, about antiquarian words and names; as that *by* meant town, and *by-laws* town-laws; *wick* meant the corner of the mouth, such names as Berwick being given to places on creeks so shaped; *glead* meant hawk, and Gladstone was Hawkstone, and so on. When the ladies had retired, Carlyle asked me to go with him to his room in order to consult a little about the revision of his address for the press. This being arranged for, he lit his pipe and fell into a long, deep silence. In the reverie every furrow passed away from his face; all anxieties seemed far away. I saw his countenance as I had never seen it before—without any trace of spiritual pain. The pathetic expression was overlaid by a sort of quiet gladness—like the soft evening glow under which the Profile on the New England mountain appears to smile; there fell on this great jutting brow and grave face, whose very laughter was often volcanic as its wrath, a sweet childlike look. He was, indeed, thinking of his childhood.

"It seems very strange," he said, "as I look back over it all now—so far away—and the faces that grew aged, and then vanished. A greater debt I owe to my father than he lived long enough to have fully paid to him. He was a very thoughtful and earnest kind of man, even to sternness. He was fond of reading, too, particularly the reading of theology. Old John Owen, of the seventeenth century, was his favorite author. He could not tolerate anything fictitious in books, and sternly forbade us to spend our time over the 'Arabian Nights'—'those downright lies,' he called them. He was grimly religious. I remember him going into the kitchen, where some servants were dancing, and reminding them very emphatically that they were dancing on

the verge of a place which no politeness ever prevented *his* mentioning on fit occasion. He himself
walked as a man in the full presence of heaven and
hell and the day of judgment. They were always
imminent. One evening, some people were playing
cards in the kitchen when the bake-house caught
fire; the events were to him as cause and effect, and
henceforth there was a flaming handwriting on our
walls against all cards. All of which was the hard
outside of a genuine veracity and earnestness of
nature such as I have not found so common among
men as to think of them in him without respect.

"My mother stands in my memory as beautiful
in all that makes the excellence of woman. Pious
and gentle she was, with an unweariable devotedness
to her family; a loftiness of moral aim and religious
conviction which gave her presence and her humble
home a certain graciousness, and, even as I see it
now, dignity; and with it, too, a good deal of wit
and originality of mind. No man ever had better
opportunities than I for comprehending, were they
comprehensible, the great deeps of a mother's love
for her children. Nearly my first profound impressions in this world are connected with the death of
an infant sister—an event whose sorrowfulness was
made known to me in the inconsolable grief of my
mother. For a long time she seemed to dissolve in
tears—only tears. For several months not one night

CARLYLE'S MOTHER.

passed but she dreamed of holding her babe in her arms, and clasping it to her breast. At length one morning she related a change in her dream: while she held the child in her arms it had seemed to break up into small fragments, and so crumbled away and vanished. From that night her vision of the babe and dream of clasping it never returned.

"The only fault I can remember in my mother was her being too mild and peaceable for the planet she lived in. When I was sent to school, she piously enjoined on me that I should, under no conceivable circumstances, fight with any boy, nor resist any evil done to me; and her instructions were so solemn

that for a long time I was accustomed to submit to
every kind of injustice, simply for her sake.   It was
a sad mistake.   When it was practically discovered
that I would not defend myself, every kind of indig-
nity was put upon me, and my life was made utterly
miserable.   Fortunately the strain was too great.
One day a big boy was annoying me, when it occurred to my mind that existence under such con-
ditions was not supportable; so I slipped off my
wooden clog, and therewith suddenly gave that boy
a blow on the seat of honor which sent him sprawl-
ing on face and stomach in a convenient mass of
mud and water.   I shall never forget the burthen
that rolled off me at that moment.   I never had a
more heart-felt satisfaction than in witnessing the
consternation of that contemporary.   It proved to
be a measure of peace, also; from that time I was
troubled by the boys no more."

Carlyle's mother died in 1853.   Dr. John Carlyle told me that although the subjects upon which
Thomas wrote were to a large extent foreign to her,
she read all of his works published up to the time of
her death with the utmost care; and his "History
of the French Revolution," particularly, she read
and reread until she had comprehended it.   With a
critical acumen known only to mothers, she excepted
"Wilhelm Meister" from her pious reprobation of
novel-reading (not failing, however, to express de-

cided opinions concerning the moral character of Philina and others). At first she was somewhat disturbed by the novel religious views encountered in these books, but she found her son steadfast and earnest, and cared for no more. I have heard that it was to her really inquiring mind that Carlyle owed his first questioning of the conventional English opinion of the character of Cromwell.

There was something indescribably touching and even thrilling in the tones of passionate longing with which Carlyle spoke of his parents. It was a Lord Rector talking about poor and comparatively ignorant workpeople long dead, but there was a love in Carlyle passing the love of women: at that moment he would have flung to the winds all the honors which the world had heaped upon him for one more day in the old home at Scotsbrig with his father— one hour of the old nestling at the heart of his mother. So long as either of them lived, he (as I knew on good information) had been constant in his pleadings for permission to contribute something to make their age happier; but they needed only his love, and they chose well—a treasure not measurable.

"As I was compelled," continued Carlyle, "to quietly abandon my mother's non-resistant lessons, so I had to modify my father's rigid rulings against books of fiction. I remember few happier days than those in which I ran off into the fields to read

'Roderick Random,' and how inconsolable I was
that I could not get the second volume. To this day
I know of few writers equal to Smollett. Humphry
Clinker is precious to me now as he was in those
years. Nothing by Dante or any one else surpasses
in pathos the scene where Humphry goes into the
smithy made for him in the old house, and whilst
he is heating the iron, the poor woman who has lost
her husband, and is deranged, comes and talks to
him as to her husband. 'John, they told me you
were dead. How glad I am you have come!' And
Humphry's tears fall down and bubble on the hot
iron.

"Ah, well, it would be a long story. As with
every 'studious boy' of that time and region, the
destiny prepared for me was the nearly inevitable
kirk. And so I came here to Edinburgh, about fourteen, and went to hard work. And still harder work
it was when the University had been passed by, the
hardest being to find work. Nearly the only companion I had was poor Edward Irving, then one of
the most attractive of youths; we had been to the
same Annan school, but he was three years my senior.
Here, and for a long time after, destiny threw us a
good deal together."

(An old Scotch gentleman who knew the two in
those Edinburgh years told me that both were vehemently argumentative; also that though Carlyle was

the better reasoner, Irving generally got the best of the argument, since he was apt to knock Carlyle down with his fist when himself driven into logical distress. This was humorously said, and no doubt a slight exaggeration of the facts.)

"Very little help did I get from anybody in those years, and, as I may say, no sympathy at all in all this old town. And if there was any difference, it was found least where I might most have hoped for it. There was Professor —— For years I attended his lectures, in all weathers and all hours. Many and many a time, when the class was called together, it was found to consist of one individual—to wit, of him now speaking; and still oftener, when others were present, the only person who had at all looked into the lesson assigned was the same humble individual. I remember no instance in which these facts elicited any note or comment from that instructor. He once requested me to translate a mathematical paper, and I worked through it the whole of one Sunday, and it was laid before him, and it was received without remark or thanks. After such long years I came to part with him, and to get my certificate. Without a word, he wrote on a bit of paper: 'I certify that Mr. Thomas Carlyle has been in my class during his college course, and has made good progress in his studies.' Then he rang a bell, and ordered a servant to open the front door for me.

Not the slightest sign that I was a person whom he could have distinguished in any crowd. And so I parted from old —— ——."

Carlyle's extraordinary attainments were clearly enough recognized by his fellow-students, among whom, no doubt, he might have found sympathetic friends had he been willing to spare time from the books he was devouring in such vast quantities. When he had graduated, the professors began to realize that their best student had gone. For two years (1814–16) he was mathematical teacher in the grammar-school at Annan, where he had been a pupil between 1806 and 1809. Then Professor Leslie, the coadjutor and afterwards the successor of Playfair, procured for him, as he had previously done for Irving, a situation as teacher in the neighborhood.

"It had become increasingly clear to me that I could not enter the ministry with any honesty of mind; and nothing else then offering, to say nothing of the utter mental confusion as to what thing was desired, I went away to that lonely straggling town on the Frith of Forth, Kirkcaldy, possessing then, as still, few objects interesting to any one not engaged in the fishing profession. Two years there of hermitage, loneliness, at the end of which something must be done. Back to Edinburgh, and for a time a small subsistence is obtained by teaching a few pupils, while the law is now the object aimed at.

Then came the dreariest years—eating of the heart, misgivings as to whether there shall be presently anything else to eat, disappointment of the nearest and dearest as to the hoped-for entrance on the ministry, and steadily growing disappointment of self with the undertaken law profession—above all, perhaps, wanderings through mazes of doubt, perpetual questionings unanswered."

"I had gradually become a devout reader in German literature, and even now began to feel a capacity for work, but heard no voice calling for just the kind of work I felt capable of doing. The first break of gray light in this kind was brought by my old friend David Brewster. He set me to work on the "Edinburgh Encyclopædia;" there was not much money in it, but a certain drill, and, still better, a sense of accomplishing something, though far yet from what I was aiming at; as, indeed, it has always been far enough from *that*."

I may recall here an occasion when Carlyle was speaking, in his stormy way, of the tendency of the age to spend itself in talk. Mrs. Carlyle (with her wonted tact, anticipating any possible suggestion of the same from some listener) said, archly, "And how about Mr. Carlyle?" He paused some moments: the storm was over, and I almost fancied that for once I saw a tear gather in the old man's eyes as he said, in low tone, "Mr. Carlyle looked long and anxiously to find something he could do with any kind of veracity: he found no door open save that he took, and had to take, though it was by no means what he would have selected." Once, too, when some vigorous person was praising a favorite poet, Carlyle spoke of the said poet as a "phrasemonger." The other, somewhat nettled, said, "But what are the best of us but phrasemongers!" Siegfried was never more conscious of the vulnerable point left by the leaf on his back than Carlyle of the distance between his doctrine of silence and his destiny of authorship. He bowed and said, "True;" and the conversation proceeded amiably enough.

Between the years 1820–24 Carlyle wrote for the "Edinburgh Encyclopædia" sixteen articles—namely, Mary Wortley Montagu, Montaigne, Montesquieu, Montfaucon, Dr. Moore, Sir John Moore, Necker, Nelson, Netherlands, Newfoundland, Norfolk, Northamptonshire, Northumberland, Mungo Park, Lord Chatham, William Pitt. To the *New Edinburgh Review*, in the same years, he contributed a paper on Joanna Baillie's "Metrical Legends," and one on Goethe's "Faust." In 1822 he made the translation of Legendre, and wrote the valuable essay on "Proportion" prefixed to it, though it did not appear until 1824. M. Louis Blanc informed me that he once met with a French treatise devoted to the discussion of the mathematical theses of Carlyle, the writer of which seemed unaware of his author's fame in other matters.

"And now" (towards the close of his twenty-seventh year this would be) "things brightened a little. Edward Irving, then amid his worshippers in London, had made the acquaintance of a wealthy family, the Bullers, who had a son with whom all teachers had effected nothing. There were two boys, and he named me as likely to succeed with them. It was in this way that I came to take charge of Charles Buller —afterwards my dear friend, Thackeray's friend also —and I gradually managed to get him ready for Cambridge. Charles and I came to love each other dearly, and we all saw him with pride steadily rising in Parliamentary distinction, when he died. Poor Charles! he was one of the finest youths I ever knew. The engagement ended without regret, but while it lasted was the means of placing me in circumstances of pecuniary comfort beyond what I had previously known, and of thus giving me the means of doing more congenial work, such as the 'Life of Schiller,' and 'Wilhelm Meister's Wanderjahre.' But one gaunt form had been brought to my side by the strain through which I had passed, who was not in a hurry to quit—ill-health. The reviewers were not able to make much of Wilhelm. De Quincey and Jeffrey looked hard at us. I presently met De Quincey, and he looked pale and uneasy, possibly thinking that he was about to encounter some resentment from the individual whom he had been cutting up. But it had made the very smallest impression upon me, and I was quite-prepared to listen respectfully to anything he had to say. And, as I remember, he made himself quite agreeable when his nervousness was gone. He had a melodious voice and an affable manner, and his powers of conversation were unusual. He had a soft, courteous way of taking up what you had said, and furthering it apparently; and you presently discovered that he didn't agree with you at all, and was quietly upsetting your positions one after another."

The review of "Wilhelm Meister" by Jeffrey, just mentioned, was one of the notable literary events of the time. Beginning his task with the foregone conclusion that prevailed at Holland House concerning all importations from Germany, even before they were visible, Jeffrey pronounced "Wilhelm Meister" to be "eminently absurd, puerile, incongruous, and affected," "almost from beginning to end one flagrant offence against every principle of taste and every rule of composition." Unfortunately, this was preceded by the statement that the judgment was made "after the most deliberate consideration;" for in the latter part of the review the writer is compelled to regard the translator "as one who has proved by his preface to be a person of talents, and by every part

of the work to be no ordinary master of at least one
of the languages with which he has to deal;" and,
finally, this strange review (this time evidently "after
the most deliberate consideration") winds up with
its confession: "Many of the passages to which we
have now alluded are executed with great talent,
and, we are very sensible, are better worth extracting
than those we have cited. But it is too late now to
change our selections, and we can still less afford to
add to them. On the whole, we close the book with
some feeling of mollification towards its faults, and
a disposition to abate, if possible, some part of the
censure we were impelled to bestow on it at the beginning."

"And now" (to resume my notes of Carlyle's
story) "an event which had for a long time been
visible as a possibility drew on to consummation. In
the loneliest period of my later life here in Edinburgh there was within reach one home and one
family to which again Irving—always glad to do me
a good turn—had introduced me.* At Haddington
lived the Welshes, and there I had formed a friendship with Jane, now Mrs. Carlyle. She was charac-

---

* Irving has left an intimation that he himself was a lover of Jane
Welsh. Carlyle's marriage took place, after a long engagement, in
1826. She was a very brilliant writer, as her letters will show when
published. She wrote a little story called "Watch and Canary;"
and, it is said, had just set to work on a novel when she died.

terized at that time by an earnest desire for knowledge, and I was for a long time aiding and directing
her studies. The family were very grateful, and
made it a kind of home for me. But when, further
on, our marriage was spoken of, the family—not un-
naturally, perhaps, mindful of their hereditary dignity (they were descended from John Knox)—opposed
us rather firmly. But Jane Welsh, having taken her
resolution, showed further her ability to defend it
against all comers; and she maintained it to the
extent of our presently dwelling man and wife at
Comley Bank (Edinburgh), and then at the old solitary farm-house called Craigenputtoch, that is, Hill
of the Hawk. The sketch of it in Goethe's translation of my 'Schiller' was made by George Moir, a
lawyer here in Edinburgh, of whom I used to see
something. The last time I saw old Craigenputtoch
it filled me with sadness—a kind of Valley of Jehoshaphat. Probably it was through both the struggles
of that time, the end of them being not yet, and the
happy events with which it was associated—now
buried and gone. It was there, and on our way
there, that the greetings and gifts of Goethe over-
took us; and it was there that Emerson found us.
He came from Dumfries in an old rusty gig; came
one day and vanished the next. I had never heard
of him: he gave us his brief biography, and told us
of his bereavement in loss of his wife. We took a

walk while dinner was prepared. We gave him a welcome, we were glad to see him: our house was homely, but she who presided there made it of neatness such as were at any moment suitable for a visit from any majesty. I did not then adequately recognize Emerson's genius; but my wife and I both thought him a beautiful transparent soul, and he was always a very pleasant object to us in the distance. Now and then a letter comes from him, and amid all the smoke and mist of this world it is always as a window flung open to the azure. During all this last weary work of mine, his words have been nearly the only ones about the thing done—'Friedrich'—to which I have inwardly responded, '*Yes—yes—yes;* and much obliged to you for saying that same!' The other day I was staying with some people who talked about some books that seemed to me idle enough; so I took up Emerson's 'English Traits,' and soon found myself lost to everything else—wandering amid all manner of sparkling crystals and wonderful luminous vistas; and it really appeared marvellous how people can read what they sometimes do with such books on their shelves. Emerson has gone a very different direction from any in which I can see my way to go; but words cannot tell how I prize the old friendship formed there on Craigenputtoch hill, or how deeply I have felt in all he has written the same aspiring intelligence which shone

about us when he came as a young man, and left
with us a memory always cherished.

"After Emerson left us, gradually all determining
interests drew us to London; and there the main
work, such as it is, has been done; and now they
have brought me down here, and got the talk out of
me!"

But here I must take a longer pause. Much did
Carlyle say here which I cannot even try to report.
He spake not to me, but as if unaware of any one's
presence; as if conversing with the risen shades of
a world I knew not. But, so often as I have read
"Sartor Resartus" since then, I have seen here and
there the man at whose feet I was then sitting;
most of all have I seen and heard the man of that
quiet chamber in Edinburgh in the weird experience
that closes "the everlasting No." That passage is a
transcript from the life of Thomas Carlyle, and summing-up of the years which preceded and ended that
final venture (i. e., the Law), to enter upon some
conventional work of the world. I will ask my
reader to ponder the words to which I have referred,
and venture to quote here:

"'So had it lasted,' concludes the Wanderer—'so
had it lasted, as in bitter protracted Death-agony,
through long years. The heart within me, unvisited
by any heavenly dew-drop, was smouldering in sul-

phurous, slow-consuming fire. Almost since earliest memory I shed no tear; or once only when I, murmuring half-audibly, recited Faust's Death-song, that wild *Selig der den er im Siegesglanze findet* (Happy whom *he* finds in Battle's splendor), and thought that of this last Friend even I was not forsaken, that Destiny itself could not doom me not to die. Having no hope, neither had I any definite fear, were it of Man or of Devil; nay, I often felt as if it might be solacing, could the Arch - devil himself, though in Tartarean terrors, but rise to me, that I might tell him a little of my mind. And yet, strangely enough, I lived in a continual, indefinite pining fear; tremulous, pusillanimous, apprehensive of I know not what: it seemed as if all things in the heavens above and the earth beneath would hurt me; as if the heavens and the earth were but boundless jaws of a devouring monster, wherein I, palpitating, waited to be devoured.

"'Full of such humor, and perhaps the miserablest man in the whole French Capital or Suburbs, was I, one sultry Dog-day, after much perambulation, toiling along the dirty little Rue Saint-Thomas de l'Enfer, among civic rubbish enough, in a close atmosphere, and over pavements hot as Nebuchadnezzar's Furnace, whereby, doubtless, my spirits were little cheered, when all at once there rose a Thought in me, and I asked myself: "What art thou afraid of? Wherefore, like a coward, dost thou forever pip and whimper, and go cowering and trembling? Despicable biped! what is the sum-total of the worst that lies before thee! Death? Well, Death; and say the pangs of Tophet too, and all that the Devil and Man may, will, or can do against thee. Hast thou not a heart? canst thou not suffer whatsoever it be? and as a Child of Freedom, though outcast, trample Tophet itself under thy feet, while it consumes thee? Let it come, then; I will meet it and defy it!" And as I so thought, there rushed like a stream of fire over my whole soul; and I shook base Fear away from me forever. I was strong, of unknown strength; a spirit, almost a god. Ever from that time the temper of my misery was changed: not Fear or whining Sorrow was it, but Indignation and grim-eyed Defiance.

"'Thus had the EVERLASTING No (*das ewige Nein*) pealed authoritatively through all the recesses of my Being, of my Me; and then it was that my whole Me stood up, in native God-created majesty, and with emphasis recorded its Protest. Such a Protest, the most important transaction in life, may that Indignation and Defiance, in a psychological point of view, be fitly called. The Everlasting No had said, "Behold, thou art fatherless, outcast, and the Universe is mine (the Devil's)," to which my whole Me now made answer, "*I* am not thine, but Free, and forever hate thee!"

" 'It is from this hour that I incline to date my Spiritual New-birth, or Baphometic Fire-baptism ; perhaps I directly thereupon began to be a Man.' "

This walk in Paris must not be supposed allegorical. Carlyle told me that it actually stood in his life as it is written in his book. He had not heard the story of how this Rue de l'Enfer came by its name until I encountered it while writing my "Demonology." In the time of Saint Louis it was a road supposed to be haunted by a fearful green monster, the Diable Vauvert, a dragon-man, who twisted the necks of all he met. It would appear to have been a phantasm got up by a murderous band of money-coiners, who occupied the ancient Château Vauvert. The Carthusian monks having offered to exorcise the devils if Saint Louis would give them the château, that was done. The Diable Vauvert left his trail only in the name of the street, now called Rocherau-Enfer. Near-by is the convent Saint Michael. But the only real dragon-slayer from the time of Saint Louis until now who has passed that way was the young Scotchman who there laid low the phantasm of Fear with the poised spear of a free mind.

One of the sorrowful days of that period was that on which he was compelled to open an abyss between himself and Edward Irving. On a long walk they sat down together, and Carlyle unfolded to him, as well as he could to a man who could so little com-

prehend them, the intellectual experiences which
forbade his entering on the ministry. They parted
to go their several ways. But Carlyle never lost his
love for his early friend; even when Irving was far
gone in insanity, he visited him and tried to soothe
him. "Friendliness still beamed in his eyes," he
wrote, "but now from amid unquiet fire; his face
was flaccid, wasted, unsound; hoary as with extreme
age: he was trembling over the brink of the grave.
Adieu, thou first friend—adieu, while this confused
twilight of existence lasts!"

## IV.

When I left Mr. Erskine's house that night, it was
to go to the office of the *Scotsman*, in order to revise
the proof of the new Lord Rector's address. Carlyle placed in my hands the notes he had made beforehand for the occasion, saying, as he did so, that
he did not suppose they would assist me much. His
surmise proved unhappily true. The notes had been
written partly in his own hand, partly by an amanuensis. Those written by the amanuensis had been
but little followed in the address, and those added
by himself were nearly undecipherable. Already
that tremor which so long affected his hand when
he held a pen—it was much steadier when he used a
pencil—afflicted him. The best-written sentences in
the notes (now before me) are the lines of Goethe

But heard are the voices,
Heard are the Sages,
The Worlds and the Ages:
"Choose well, your choice is
Brief and yet endless.

"Here eyes do regard you
In Eternity's stillness,
Here is all fullness,
Ye brave, to reward you;
Work, and despair not."

FAC-SIMILE OF CARLYLE'S HANDWRITING.

which he repeated at the close of the address, a facsimile of which I give.

For the rest, I find in these notes (which, on my request, he said I was welcome to keep) some passages which were not spoken, but were meant to reach the public. I therefore quote them here, premising only that where I have supplied more than a connecting word, such phrase is put in brackets, and mainly supplied from what he really did say.

### EXTRACTS FROM THE NOTES.

"Beautiful is young enthusiasm; keep it to the end, and be more and more correct in fixing on the object of it. It is a terrible thing to be wrong in that—the source of all our miseries and confusions whatever."

"The 'Seven Liberal Arts' notion of education is now a little obsolete; but try whatever is set before you; gradually find what is fittest for *you*. This you will learn to read in all sciences and subjects."

"You will not learn it from any current set of History Books; but God has *not* gone to sleep, and eternal Justice, not eternal Vulpinism [is the law of the universe]."

"It was for religion that universities were first instituted; practically for that, under all changes of dialect, they continue: pious awe of the Great Unknown makes a sacred canopy, under which all has to grow. All is lost and futile in universities if that fail. Sciences and technicalities are very good and useful, indeed, but in comparison they are as adjuncts to the smith's shop."

"There is in this university a considerable stir about endowments. That there should be need of such is not honorable to us at a time when so many in Scotland and elsewhere have suddenly become pos-

sessed of millions which they do not know what to do with. Like
that Lancashire gentleman who left a quarter of a million to help pay
the national debt. Poor soul! All he had got in a life of toil and
struggle were certain virtues — diligence, frugality, endurance, patience—truly an invaluable item, but an invisible one. The money
which secured all was strictly zero! I am aware, all of us are aware,
a little money is needed; but there are limits to the need of money—
comparatively altogether narrow limits. To every mortal in this stu-
pendous universe incalculably higher objects than money! The deep-
est depths of Vulgarism is that of setting up money as our Ark of the
Covenant. Devorgilla gave [a good deal of money gathered by John
Balliol in Scotland] to Balliol College in Oxford, and we don't want
it back; but as to the then ratio of man's soul to man's stomach,
man's celestial part to his terrestrial, and even bestial, compared to
the now ratio in such improved circumstances, is a reflection, if we
pursue it, that might humble us to the dust.

" [The English are the richest people, in the way of endowments, on
the face of the earth, in their universities; and it is a remarkable fact
that since the time of Bentley you cannot name anybody that has
gained a great name in scholarship among them, or constituted a
point of revolution in the pursuits of men in that way. The man
that does that is worthy of being remembered among men, though he
may be poor, not endowed with worldly wealth. One man that actually did constitute a revolution was the son of a poor weaver in Sax-
ony, who edited his 'Tibullus' in Dresden in the room of a poor
comrade, and while he was editing it had to gather peascod shells in
the street and boil them for dinner. His name was Heyne. I can
remember it was quite a revolution in my mind when I got hold of
that man's book on Virgil.] Be zealous [for learning]: far beyond
money is it to use well what is prepared for us. You cannot wait on
better times; for you, it is here and now, or else never; the better
times will come if they can.

" We have ceased to believe, as Devorgilla did, that in colleges and
monasteries is the certain road to Wisdom; and, alas! secondly, that

Wisdom is the way to heaven. Many of us think—do they not? though nobody will say so—that cent. per cent. is the real course that leads to advantages. In regard to the colleges and monasteries, I agree with all the world in considerably dissenting from Devorgilla. Wisdom is not quite so certainly to be obtained there; but in regard to the second proposition, I do go with her, and invite every living soul to go with her—that Wisdom is, was, and to the end of time and through eternity will be, the supreme object for a man, and the only path upward for his objects and for him. Yes, my friends, especially you, my young friends, that is forever the divine thing for us; whatever heaven we can expect, there, or nowhere, is the road to it. [In Wisdom, 'namely, sound appreciation and just decision as to all the objects that come round about you, and the habit of behaving with justice and wisdom.'] I would have you reflect much upon this, mostly in silence, in all stages of your life-journey, in all scenes and situations; the more purely you can discern that, and the more steadfastly act upon it, the better it will be for you. On other terms, victory is possible for no man.

"Silent Wisdom! The mute ages, they say nothing for themselves; but in this, the object and centre of all articulate knowledge, one has to call them far more opulent. The old Baron who had no literature whatever, could not sign his name, had to put his cross mark, sometimes dipped his iron hand and stamped that—many a 'brilliant' writing and what not seems to me the reverse of improvement on him! Noble virtues dwelt in him, spotless honor in interests not to be measured in worldly good; an authentic commerce with heaven not at all recognizable in his witty descendant. Prudent, patient, valiant, steering towards his object with all the qualities needful, and his object a good one, one begins to see in him what the real History of England was—the making of the best men. And so it lasted for six or seven generations. When you once put speech into that, it is a glorious thing—glorious to the wise man himself, and to all the world. But let me remind you, you may superadd speech, and unfortunately have little or nothing of all that to superadd it to. A man may actually have no wisdom, and be a very great talker. How to regain all that? You will regain it in proportion as you are sincere. I often hear of an "excellent speech;" well, but it is the existence of the things spoken that will benefit me. So much depends on a man's morality; on the heart fully as much depends as on the head—the Heart is first of all! There are 75,000 sermons preached every Sunday—dry-rot; but I will not suppose you gone into that state. It is a long road I have travelled, and you are all upon it, struggling forward into the undiscovered country, which to your fathers and grandfathers is but too well known; surely if they would speak to you with candor and sincerity and insight, they might throw some light on it.

"If all this is the supreme end of universities, it becomes more and more dubious of attainment therein. The old Baron learned by apprenticeship; theoretic instruction will not do; it is a dreadful case when the theoretic is got, and the real missed. This has led some to think of *mute* education."

"What is fame? Shakespeare ends with, 'Good friend, for Jesus' sake, forbear!'"

"Much confusion you may count on ahead, but there are beneficent hearts too: their doors may seem closed; but such you will find, and their human love of you and help of you will be balm for all your wounds."

In transmitting a report of Carlyle's address as Lord Rector to the *Pall Mall Gazette,* I wrote a note, which was printed in that journal, and which I venture to insert here: "I have never heard a speech of whose more remarkable qualities so few can be conveyed on paper. You will read of 'applause' and 'laughter,' but you will little realize the eloquent blood flaming up the speaker's cheek, the kindling of his eye, or the inexpressible voice and look when the drolleries were coming out. When he spoke of clap-trap books exciting astonishment 'in the minds of foolish persons,' the evident halting at the word 'fools,' and the smoothing of his hair, as if he must be decorous, which preceded the 'foolish persons,' were exceedingly comical. As for the flaming bursts, they took shape in grand tones, whose impression was made deeper, not by raising, but by lowering the voice. Your correspondent here declares that he should hold it worth his coming all the way from London in the rain in the Sunday-night train were it only to have heard Carlyle say, 'There is a nobler ambition than the gaining of all California, or the getting of all the suffrages that are on the planet just now.' In the first few minutes of the address there was some hesitation, and much of the shrinking that one might expect in a secluded scholar; but these very soon cleared away, and during the larger part, and to the close of the oration, it was evident that he was receiving a sympathetic influence from his listeners, which he did not fail to return tenfold. The applause became less frequent; the silence became that of a woven spell; and the recitation of the beautiful lines from Goethe at the end was so masterly, so marvellous, that one felt in it that Carlyle's real anathemas against rhetoric were but the expression of his knowledge that there is a rhetoric beyond all other arts."

## V.

On the evening of the Edinburgh Address, I wrote
to Mrs. Carlyle, giving particulars concerning Carlyle and the installation which I knew she would be
glad to hear. Alas! alas! It was but a few weeks
after that I placed in Carlyle's hand, when he returned from her grave, the answer to my letter—one
of the last she ever wrote. Here it is:

"5 Cheyne Row, Chelsea, 5 *April*, 1866.

"My dear Mr. Conway,—The 'disposition to write me a little
note,' was a good inspiration, and I thank you for it; or rather, ac-
cepting it as an inspiration, I thank Providence for it—Providence,
'Immortal Gods,' 'Superior Powers,' 'Destinies,' whichever be the
name you like best.

"Indeed, by far the most agreeable part of this flare-up of success,
to my feeling, has been the enthusiasm of personal affection and sympathy on the part of his friends. I haven't been so fond of everybody, and so pleased with the world, since I was a girl, as just in
these days when reading the letters of his friends, your own included.
I am not very well, having done what I do at every opportunity—
gone off my sleep; so I am preparing to spend a day and night at
Windsor for change of atmosphere, moral as well as material. I am
in a hurry, but couldn't refrain from saying, 'Thank you, and all
good be with you!'

"Sincerely yours,     Jane W. Carlyle."

"Whatever 'triumph' there may have been," said
Carlyle, when I next met him, "in that now so darkly overcast day, was indeed *hers*. Long, long years

ago, she took her place by the side of a poor man of humblest condition, against all other provisions for her, undertook to share his lot for weal or woe; and in that office what she has been to him and done for him, how she has placed, as it were, velvet between him and all the sharp angularities of existence, remains now only in the knowledge of one man, and will presently be finally hid in his grave."

Nothing could be more beautiful than the loving reverence of Carlyle for the delicate, soft-voiced little lady whose epitaph he wrote in words that may here be quoted:

"Here likewise now rests Jane Welsh Carlyle, spouse of Thomas Carlyle, Chelsea, London. She was born at Haddington, 14th July, 1801, only child of the above John Welsh and of Grace Welsh, Caplegell, Dumfriesshire, his wife. In her bright existence she had more sorrows than are common, but also a soft invincibility, a capacity of discernment, and a noble loyalty of heart, which are rare. For forty years she was the true and loving helpmate of her husband, and by act and word unweariedly forwarded him as none else could in all of worthy that he did or attempted. She died at London, 21st April, 1866, suddenly snatched away from him, and the light of his life as if gone out."

When Carlyle's mood was stormiest, her voice could in an instant allay it; the lion was led as by a little child. She sat a gentle invalid on the sofa, and in the end, whatever had been the outburst of indignation, justice was sure to be done, and the mitigation sure to be remembered. I can hear her voice

now—" But, Mr. Carlyle, you remember he did act
very nobly towards that poor man," etc., followed
from the just now Rhadamanthus with, " Ah, yes;
he had, after all, a vein of good feeling in him;" and
then came the neatest summing-up of virtues concerning some personage whose fragments we had
despaired of ever picking up. Carlyle was always
modest when speaking of himself—which he rarely
did—and artistic in his portraits of others. The
shades might be laid on rather thickly at first, but
the lights were sure to be added at each possible
point,—except, indeed, in the case of a few typical
public figures, to hate whom was in the essence of
his religion. Mrs. Carlyle had a true poetic nature
and an almost infallible insight. In the conversation
which went on in the old drawing-room at Chelsea
there was no suggestion of things secret or reserved;
people with sensitive toes had no careful provision
made for them, and had best keep away; free, frank,
and simple speech and intercourse were the unwrit-
ten but ever-present law. Mrs. Carlyle's wit and
humor were overflowing, and she told anecdotes
about her husband under which he sat with a patient look of repudiation until the loud laugh broke
out and led the chorus. Now it was when she described his work on " Friedrich " as one of those
botanical growths which every now and then come
to a knot, which being slowly passed, it grows on

CHOIR OF ABBEY CHURCH, HADDINGTON, MRS. CARLYLE'S GRAVE IN THE FOREGROUND.

to another knot. "What Mr. Carlyle is when one of those knots is reached, must be left to vivid imaginations." Again it was a transitory cook who served up daily some mess described by Carlyle as "Stygian," with "Tartarean" for a variant. She being dismissed, another applicant comes.

"Carlyle having, you are aware, deep intuitive insight into human character, goes down to speak to the new woman, and returns to pronounce her a most worthy and honest person. The woman next comes to me, and a more accomplished Sairey Gamp my eyes never looked on. The great coarse creature comes close, eyes me from head to foot, and begins by telling me, 'When people dies, I can lay 'em out perfect.' 'Sairey' was not retained, though I had no doubt whatever of her ability to lay any of us out 'perfect.'"

One evening the talk fell on the Brownings. Carlyle had given us the most attractive picture of Robert Browning in his youth. "He had simple speech and manners, and ideas of his own; and I recall a very pleasing talk with him during a walk, somewhere about Croydon, to the top of a hill. Miss Barrett sent me some of her first verses in manuscript, and I wrote back that I thought she could do better than write verses. But then she wrote again, saying: 'What else can I do? Here am I chained to my sofa by disease.' I wrote then, taking back all

I had said. Her father was a physician, late from
India; a harsh impracticable man, as I have heard,
his lightest word standing out like laws of the Medes
and Persians. One day she read some verses Browning had written about her." "Oh no," interrupts
Mrs. Carlyle, "she wrote something about Browning." "Ah, well," continues Carlyle, "you shall give
the revised and corrected edition presently. As I
was saying, she wrote something about him, compar-
ing him to some fruit—" "Oh, Mr. Carlyle!" ex-
claims Mrs. C. "She compared him," continues Carlyle, "to a nectarine." "That's too bad," says Mrs.
Carlyle; "she compared his poetry to a pomegranate
—it was suggested by the title of his poems, "Bells
and Pomegranates:

"'And from Browning some pomegranate which, cut deep down the
      middle,
   Shows a heart within blood-tinctured with a veined humanity.'"

"I stand corrected," says Carlyle, "and the lines are
very sweet and true;" and he then proceeded to tell
the pleasant romance on which he set out with a subtle appreciation and sympathetic admiration which
made it sweeter than the tale of the Sleeping Beauty.

The advice which Carlyle gave to Miss Barrett,
and which so many will rejoice that she did not follow, but induced him to take back, was characteristic.
That Carlyle was himself a poet all his true readers
know; had his early life been happier, it is even

probable that he might have broken upon the world with songs such as his "Tragedy of the Night-moth" and "Here hath been dawning another blue day" show him to have been amply able to sing; but his ideal was too literally a *burden* to rise with full freedom on its wings. He could rarely or never read the rhymes of his contemporaries — Goethe always excepted—without a sense of some frivolity in that mode of expression. The motto of "Past and Present," from Schiller—"Ernst ist das Leben"—was deeply graven on Carlyle's heart. Thomas Cooper, author of the "Purgatory of Suicides" (dedicated to Carlyle), like so many others who had suffered for their efforts for reform, was befriended by Carlyle. "Twice," says Cooper, in his Autobiography, "he put a five-pound note in my hand when I was in difficulties, and told me, with a grave look of humor, that if I could never pay him again he would not hang me." Carlyle gave Cooper more than money— a copy of "Past and Present," and therewith some excellent advice. The letter is fine, and my reader will be glad to read it.

"CHELSEA, *September* 1, 1845.

"DEAR SIR,—I have received your poem, and will thank you for that kind gift, and for all the friendly sentiments you entertain towards me—which, as from an evidently sincere man, whatever we may think of them otherwise, are surely valuable to a man. I have looked into your poem, and find indisputable traces of genius in it—a dark

3*

Titanic energy struggling there, for which we hope there will be a clearer daylight by-and-by. If I might presume to advise, I think I would recommend you to try your next work in *Prose*, and as a thing turning altogether on *Facts*, not Fictions. Certainly the *music* that is very traceable here might serve to irradiate into harmony far profitabler things than what are commonly called 'Poems,' for which, at any rate, the taste in these days seems to be irrevocably in abeyance. We have too horrible a practical chaos round us, out of which every man is called by the birth of him to make a bit of *Cosmos*; that seems to me the real Poem for a man — especially at present. I always grudge to see any portion of a man's *musical talent* (which is the real intellect, the real vitality or life of him) expended on making mere words rhyme. These things I say to all my poetic friends, for I am in earnest about them; but get almost nobody to believe me hitherto. From you I shall get an excuse at any rate, the purpose·of my so speaking being a friendly one towards you.

"I will request you, further, to accept this book of mine, and to appropriate what you can of it. 'Life is a serious thing,' as Schiller says, and as you yourself practically know. These are the words of a serious man about it; they will not altogether be without meaning for you."

Those who have read the "Purgatory of Suicides" will be able to understand the extent to which Carlyle was influenced by his sympathies. A man who, like Cooper, had been in jail for Chartist opinions might be pretty sure, in those days, of getting a certificate for some "traces of genius" from Carlyle. My old friend William Lovett, a working-man and a Radical, who had written a forcible letter to the English people from Warwick Jail, related to me the tenderness and warmth with which he was received by Carlyle. Indeed, the author of "Chartism" wrote his name so deep in the hearts of old Radicals that they were never able to look far enough beyond his sympathies to read his censures or his retractations.

When Carlyle came to live in London, it was with something of the same feeling that animated the Friar Bernard when he went to Rome, according to the legend so finely used by Emerson in his lecture on "The Conservative" (1841). The Friar had lamented in his cell on Mont Cenis the crimes of mankind, and went to Rome to reform the general corruption; but when he reached Rome, he was welcomed in the homes of the rich, found them loving each other, bestowing alms on the poor, trying to relieve the hard times. "Then the Friar Bernard went home swiftly with other thoughts than he brought, saying, 'This way of life is wrong; yet these Romans, whom I prayed God to destroy, are lovers, they are lovers: what can I do?'" Carlyle was disappointed in the two classes — that from which he hoped much, that from which he looked for little. As his favorite heroes had been poor men, working-men or even peasants, who had risen above all obstacles, so did he again and again cheer and help and idealize men like Thomas Cooper and Ebenezer Elliott and Samuel Bamford, seeing in them morning-stars. But these faded away, or set, without casting any great splendors over the world.

On the other hand, he found aristocratic friends, like Lansdowne and Ashburton, all alive to the evils of the time, sympathizing with the Radicals, Chartists, fighters against the Corn-laws. Carlyle's radicalism gradually faded, and in the Continental revolutions of 1848 went out altogether.

Four letters have recently been laid before the Literary and Philosophical Society of Manchester, and printed in the *Examiner* there, of which some extracts must be quoted here. They were written by Carlyle to Samuel Bamford, an old Radical who had been to prison, and had struggled by the side of Henry Hunt — idealized in George Eliot's "Felix Holt, the Radical." Bamford began a record of his experiences in a little book called "Life of a Radical," and sent a copy of it to Carlyle. It was acknowledged with enthusiasm (1843), and several copies ordered by the author at Chelsea. He wrote:

"I read your book with much interest; with a true desire to hear more and more of the authentic news of Middleton and of the honest toiling men there. Many persons have a similar desire. I would recommend you to try whether there is not yet more to be said, perhaps, on some side of that subject; for it belongs to an important class in these days. A man is at all times entitled, or even called upon by occasion, to speak and write and in all fit ways utter what he has himself gone through and known and got the mastery of; and in truth, at bottom, there is nothing else that any man has a right to write of. For the rest, one principle, I think, in whatever farther you write, may be enough to guide you: that of standing rigorously by the fact, however naked it look. Fact is eternal; all fiction is very transitory in comparison. All men are interested in any man if he will speak the facts of his life for them; his authentic experience, which corresponds, as face with face, to that of all other sons of Adam."

The letter from which this was taken was dated at Chelsea. The next letter, acknowledging a further instalment of Bamford's "Life," is written five years later, and dated at "The Grange, Hampshire," where Carlyle was staying with his aristocratic friends. In this he writes:

"There are only two precepts I will bid you, once more, always keep in mind: the first is to be brief; not to dwell on an object one instant after you have made it clear to the reader, and, on the whole, to be select in your objects taken for description, dwelling on each in proportion to its likelihood to interest, omitting many in which such likelihood is doubtful, and only bringing out the more important into prominence and detail. The second, which indeed is still more essential, but which I need not insist upon, since I see you scrupulously observe it, is to be exact to the truth in all points; never to hope to mend a fact by polishing any corner of it off into fiction, or adding any ornament which it had not, but to give it us always as God gave it—that, I suppose, will turn out to be best state it could be in! These two principles, I think, are the whole law of the matter; and, in fact, they are the epitome of what a sound, strong, and healthy mind will, by Nature, be led to achieve in such an enterprise; wherefore, perhaps, my best 'precept' of all were, to recommend Samuel Bamford to his own good genius (to his own honest good sense and healthy instincts) and bid him write or omit without misgivings whenever that had clearly spoken! And, on the whole, persevere and prosper; that is the wish we form for you.

"We are here among high people, to whom the 'Passages' and other writings of yours are known: last night I was commissioned by Lord Lansdowne, to ask you to send him a copy of this new work."

The year in which this last letter is dated (1848)
was, as I have said, that revolutionary year, in several
senses, which revolutionized Carlyle, and began his
reaction against radicalism.   As Wordsworth was
turned to his extreme conservatism by the French
Revolution—during part of which he was in Paris—
so Carlyle was repelled and disgusted by the events
of '48 on the Continent.   There is just a slight in-
dication of the change in the third letter to Bamford,
from which I give an extract as follows:

"On the whole, however, we must not yet let you off, or allow you
to persuade yourself that you have done with us.   A vast deal more
of knowledge about Lancashire operatives, and their ways of living
and thinking, their miseries and advantages, their virtues and sins,
still lies in your experience; and you must endeavor, by all good
methods, to get it winnowed, the chaff of it well separated from the
wheat, and to let us have the latter, as your convenience will serve.
To workers themselves you might have much to say, in the way of
admonition, encouragement, instruction, reproof; and the Captains
of Workers, the rich people, are very willing also to listen to you, and
certain of them will believe heartily whatever true thing you tell
them : this is a combination of auditors which nobody but yourself
has such hold of at present ; and you must encourage yourself to do
with all fidelity whatever you can in that peculiar and by no means
unimportant position you occupy.   'Brevity, sincerity'—and, in fact,
all sorts of manful virtue—will have once more, as they everywhere in
this world do, avail you."

It is very faint though—the tinge of reaction—as
yet; only a little more faith in the "Captains of
Workers," and a shade less in the workmen.   The

letter was written in January, 1849. The next is in April of the same year. In it he encloses twenty-five pounds presented by Lord Ashburton to Bamford, in whose Life that nobleman had been interested. It would seem that Bamford had written and wished to publish some poems; that was a thing Carlyle never failed to oppose. He says the publishers do not want poetry; the public will not buy it; poetry is a bugbear:

"For my own part, too, I own I had much rather see a sensible man, like you, put down your real thoughts and convictions in prose, than occupy yourself with fancies and imaginations such as are usually dealt with in verse. The time is in deadly earnest; our life itself, in all times, is a most earnest practical matter, and only incidentally a sportful or singing or rhyming one: let S. Bamford continue to tell us in fresh truthful prose the things he has learned about Lancashire and the world; that, I must say, would be my verdict too!"

So hard did Carlyle struggle to believe in the British working-men! Reading these letters, I can only once more mourn that his early difficulties did not make good their threat of sending him over to America. Thor with his hammer—and the "trip-hammer with æolian attachment," as Emerson described it—had happier work awaiting him in the New World than any he found in the Old.

When Carlyle visited Berlin, he went to a museum there. "The keeper of it," he told me, "insisted on showing me everything in the place; but what I went to see was Friedrich's clothes. It was as if one should go into an inn to take a chop, and they insisted he must eat everything in their store. Finally, after some contention, I looked upon Friedrich's military old clothes. And I saw that I really had properly nothing to do with those clothes. Considerations of self-respect, chiefly, made me undertake the 'Life of Friedrich,' but it has been all toil and pain." Carlyle's sigh as he spoke of "Friedrich's military old clothes" was more pathetic than anything in "Sartor." The hammer had done its tremendous stroke of work, but the strain of the æolian attachment was evermore in the minor key.

## VI.

Carlyle and his young wife had visited London before there was any thought of their going to reside there. In February, 1832, they were staying at No. 4 Ampton Street, Gray's Inn Road. Here one morning Carlyle received a volume addressed to the author of the essay on "Characteristics." It was acknowledged in this note:

"The writer of the essay named 'Characteristics' has just received, apparently from Mr. Leigh Hunt, a volume entitled 'Christianism,' for which he hereby begs to express his thanks. The volume shall be read: to meet the author of it personally would doubtless be a new gratification. T. CARLYLE."

The volume alluded to bore on its title-page:

"'Christianism; or, Belief and Unbelief Reconciled.' Being Exercises and Meditations. 'Mercy and Truth have met together; Righteousness and Peace have kissed each other.' Not for sale; only seventy-five copies printed. 1832." It was a book which completely captivated the heart of Carlyle. It was enlarged and published in 1853 under the title " The Religion of the Heart," but I cannot forbear offering here an extract from its preface, styled " Introductory Letter," and signed Leigh Hunt:

"To begin the day with an avowed sense of duty and a mutual cheerfulness of endeavor is at least an earnest of its being gone through with the better. The dry sense of duty, or even of kindness, if rarely accompanied with a tender expression of it, is but a formal and dumb virtue, compared with a livelier sympathy : and it misses part of its object, for it contributes so much the less to happiness. Affection loves to hear the voice of affection. Love wishes to be told that it is beloved. It is humble enough to seek in the reward of that acknowledgment the certainty of having done its duty. In the pages before you there is as much as possible of this mutual strengthening of benevolence, and as little of dogmatism. They were written in a spirit of sincerity, which would not allow a different proceeding. . . . Some virtues which have been thought of little comparative moment, such as those which tend to keep the body in health and the mind in good temper, are impressed upon the aspirant as religious duties. What virtues can be of greater consequence than those which regulate the color of the whole ground of life, and effect the greatest purposes of all virtue and all benevolence? Much is made, accordingly, not only of the bodily duties, but of the very duty of cheerfulness, and of setting a cheerful example. In a word, the whole object is to encourage everybody to be, and to make, happy; to look generously, nevertheless, on such pains, as well as pleasure, as are necessary for this purpose; to seek, as much as possible, and much more than is common, their own pleasures through the medium of those of others; to co-operate *with* heaven, instead of thinking it has made us only to mourn and be resigned; to unite in the great work of extending knowledge and education; to cultivate a reasonable industry, and an equally reasonable enjoyment; not to think gloomily of this world, because we hope for a better; not to cease to hope for a better, because we may be able to commence our heaven in this."

Carlyle was already weary of the shrill negations, albeit he had accepted many of them, and found in such thoughts and aspirations as these the expression of a congenial spirit. He had, indeed, read with admiration Leigh Hunt's previous and public works, but now he longed to know him. The brief note quoted seems to have elicited a cordial response from Leigh Hunt. Here is another note from Carlyle to Leigh Hunt, dated soon after the last quoted:

"4 AMPTON STREET,
"GRAY'S INN ROAD, 20*th February*, 1832.

"DEAR SIR,—I stay at home (scribbling) till after two o'clock, and shall be truly glad, *any* morning, to meet in person a man whom I have long, in spirit, seen and esteemed.

"Both my wife and I, however, would reckon it a still greater favor could you come at once in the evening, and take tea with us, that our interview might be the longer and freer. Might we expect you, for instance, on Wednesday night? Our hour is six o'clock; but we will alter it in any way to suit you.

"We venture to make this proposal because our stay in town is now likely to be short, and we should be sorry to miss having free speech of you. Believe me, dear sir, very sincerely yours,

"THOMAS CARLYLE."

Here, then, in a rather dingy part of London, began the lasting friendship between Carlyle and Leigh Hunt, illustrated in the letters contained in Part III. of this work.

Readers of Leigh Hunt's "Autobiography" need not be reminded of the loving reverence with which that author regarded Carlyle. "I believe," he wrote, "that what Mr. Carlyle loves better than his fault-finding, with all its eloquence, is the face of any human creature that looks suffering and loving and sincere; and I believe, further, that if the fellow-creature were suffering only, and neither loving nor sincere, but had come to a pass of agony in this life which put him at the mercies of some good man for some last help and consolation towards his grave, even at the risk of loss to repute, and a sure amount of pain and vexation, that man, if the groan reached him in its forlornness, would be Thomas Carlyle."

There is a tradition, I believe a true one, that the two chief male characters in "The Onyx Ring," by John Sterling, were meant to represent Carlyle and Goethe (Collins and Walsingham). Those who have read that charming romance will recognize in its great-hearted hero an estimate of Carlyle confirmatory of Leigh Hunt, and even more important as coming from the most intimate friend Carlyle ever had.*

---

* "Not far," said Maria, "from the point we are approaching,

It was a characteristic of Carlyle that, though he really loved but few, he never recalled his heart once given. There were many who felt that (as I once heard Mill say) "Carlyle had turned against all his

---

lives the man we have before spoken of—the hermit Collins. I have seen him often; and, strange as he is, I like him very much. There is such thorough honesty about him, as well as so much queer uncouth kindness, that he interests me extremely. He is the most marked and original figure I have ever heard of in England. Whatever is usual or commonplace among us seems to have influenced him only by contraries, and called out nothing but opposition."

"All that," answered Walsingham, "is very foolish, or at least very imperfectly wise. In every age there is good enough, if a man will put himself into harmony with it, to enable him to produce more good out of it. . . . We are not thrown down out of the sky like meteoric stones, but are formed by the same laws and gradual processes as all about us, and so are adapted to it all, and it to us. But, no doubt, Collins will fight his way through his present angry element to peace and activity. What employment has he now?"

"He minds his beehives. To the few people he ever sees, he talks quaintly and vigorously—I sometimes think, wildly; but all he says has a strong stamp upon it, and never could pass from hand to hand without notice. After having heard him, some of his phrases keep ringing in one's ears, as if he had sent a goblin trumpeter to haunt one with the sound, for days and nights after. But I have always felt that he has more in his mind than ever comes out in the expression; and, odd as his talk is, I should hardly call it affected or conceited."

"Ah! no doubt there must be much genuine nature there. But although these vehement lava-lumps and burning coals of his may be no mere showy firework, and do shoot out from a hot central furnace, I would rather it were so much cool, clear water, pouring from an inward lake of freshness."

friends," but this was only true of their radicalism, which he once shared. On the other hand, Charles Kingsley, who had shared his reaction in political affairs, kept away from him a good deal in later years because he felt himself to be one of the large number implicitly arraigned in the "Life of Sterling" as the disappointed young ladies who had taken the veil. But Carlyle always spoke affectionately of Kingsley. "I have a very vivid remembrance," he once said, "of Charles coming with his mother to see me. A lovely woman she was, with large, clear eyes, a somewhat pathetic expression of countenance, sincerely interested in all religious questions. The delicate boy she brought with her had much the same expression, and sat listening with intense and silent interest to all that was said. He was always of an eager, loving, poetic nature."

With Alfred Tennyson his frequent intercourse was interrupted when the poet went to reside in the Isle of Wight. Until then they used to sit with a

---

"I can fancy him saying—the All is right. There must be a Fire-God as well as a Water-God. If there were no fire-forces seething and blasting, for aught you know the fountains and flood-forces would stagnate into slime. . . ."

"All very true. But I stoop to drink of the stream; and I hasten away from the eruption."

"In this case," replied Maria, laughing, "the eruption saves you the trouble. It seeks no one, and loves its solitude" ("The Onyx Ring;" published in *Blackwood's Magazine*, 1838).

little circle of friends under the one tree that made the academy of the Chelsea home, smoke long pipes, and interchange long arguments. But they remained warm friends; and when Tennyson visited London, they generally met, and were very apt to relapse into the old current of conversation that had begun under the tree. I may mention here the delicacy of Carlyle towards Tennyson when they were both offered titles at the same time by Disraeli. Carlyle having written his reply declining the offer, withheld it carefully until the answer of Tennyson had been made known, fearing that the latter might in some degree be supposed to have been influenced by the course he himself had resolved to adopt.

Some of Carlyle's earlier friends had been drawn to him by the dazzling attractions of "Sartor Resartus." A contemporary writer reports of the audiences which attended the lectures on "Heroes" that "they chiefly consisted of persons of rank and wealth," and he added, "There is something in his manner which must seem very uncouth to London audiences of the most respectable class, accustomed as they are to the polished deportment which is usually exhibited in Willis's or the Hanover rooms." Not a few of these Turveydrop folk fell back when they found whither that pillar of fire was leading them.

## VII.

Dr. John Carlyle told me, with reference to the quaint framework of his brother's unique book ("Sartor Resartus"), that he had no doubt it was suggested by the accounts he (Dr. C.) used to give him of his experiences in Germany while pursuing his medical studies there. There was a Schelling Club, which Schelling himself used to visit now and then, devoted to beer, smoke, and philosophy. The free, and often wild, speculative talks of these cloud-veiled (with tobacco-smoke) intelligences of the transcendental Olympus amused his brother Thomas much in the description and rehearsal, and the doctor said he recalled many of the comments and much of the laughter in "Sartor Resartus." Apart from this framework, there never was a book which came more directly from the heart and life of a man; and being for that very reason a chapter of the world's experience, it was a word which came to its own only to find a slow reception. It was a long time before it could find a publisher—this great book into which five years of labor had gone—but at last (1833) Mr. Fraser consented to publish it in his magazine, much to the consternation of his readers.

"When it began to appear," said Carlyle, "poor Fraser, who had courageously undertaken it, found himself in great trouble. The public had no liking whatever for that kind of thing. Letters lay piled mountain high on his table, the burden of them being, 'Either stop sending your magazine to me, or stop printing that crazy stuff about clothes.' I advised him to hold on a little longer, and asked if there were no voices in a contrary sense. 'Just two —a Mr. Emerson, of New England, and a Catholic priest at Cork.' These said, 'Send me *Fraser* so long as "Sartor" continues in it.'" Some years afterwards Carlyle visited Cork, and found out his Roman Catholic reader, and he used to relate, with some drollery, how he was kept waiting for some time because the servant was unwilling to disturb him during some hours of penance and prayer with which he was engaged in the garden. "The interview did not amount to much."

"Sartor Resartus" first appeared in book form in New England (1835), edited by Emerson, to whom also is to be credited the collection of Carlyle's miscellaneous papers. Carlyle loved to dwell upon the recognition he had received from New England in the years when he was comparatively unknown in his own country. "There was really something maternal in the way America treated me. The first book I ever saw of mine, the first I could look upon as wholly my own, was sent me from that country, and I think it was the most pathetic event of my life when I saw it laid on my table. The 'French Revolution,' too, which had alarmed everybody here, and brought me no penny, was taken up in America with enthusiasm, and as much as one hundred and fifty pounds sent to me for it." "Sartor Resartus" and the "Miscellanies" were both published in England in book form in 1838, after their appearance in America.

Mr. Carlyle was much urged about that time to visit the United States, and had intended to do so; he was, I believe, only prevented from fulfilling his intention by the pressure of his labors on the "French Revolution" — more particularly by the necessity of reproducing the first volume of it, which had been burned by a servant-girl.

There is a letter of which my reader will be glad to read a portion in this memoir, and in connection with what has been said concerning the home and circumstances amid which "Sartor Resartus" was written. It is Carlyle's letter to Goethe, published in the latter's translation of the "Life of Schiller" (Frankfort, 1830):

"You inquire with such warm interest respecting our present abode and occupations, that I feel bound to say a few words about both, while there is still room left. Dumfries is a pleasant town, containing about fifteen thousand inhabitants, and may be considered the centre of the trade and judicial system of a district which possesses some importance in the sphere of Scottish industry. Our residence is not in the town itself, but fifteen miles to the northwest, among the granite hills and the black morasses which stretch westward through

4

Galloway almost to the Irish Sea. In this wilderness of heath and
rock our estate stands forth a green oasis, a tract of ploughed, partly
enclosed and planted ground, where corn ripens, and trees afford a
shade, although surrounded by sea-mews and rough-wooled sheep.
Here, with no small effort, have we built and furnished a neat, sub-
stantial dwelling; here, in the absence of professorial or other office,
we live to cultivate literature according to our strength, and in our
own peculiar way. We wish a joyful growth to the rose and flowers
of our garden; we hope for health and peaceful thoughts to further
our aims. The roses, indeed, are still in part to be planted, but they
blossom already in anticipation. Two ponies, which carry us everywhere, and the mountain air, are the best medicines for weak nerves.
This daily exercise—to which I am much devoted—is my only recre-
ation : for this nook of ours is the loveliest in Britain—six miles re-
moved from any one likely to visit me. Here Rousseau would have
been as happy as on his island of St. Pierre. My town friends, indeed, ascribe my sojourn here to a similar disposition, and forbode me
no good result. But I came hither solely with the design to simplify
my way of life, and to secure the independence through which I could
be enabled to remain true to myself. This bit of earth is our own;
here we can live, write, and think as best pleases ourselves, even
though Zoilus himself were to be crowned the monarch of literature.
Nor is the solitude of such great importance; for a stage-coach takes
us speedily to Edinburgh, which we look upon as our British Weimar.
And have I not, too, at this moment piled up upon the table of my
little library a whole cart-load of French, German, American, and
English journals and periodicals—whatever may be their worth? Of
antiquarian studies, too, there is no lack. From some of our heights
I can descry, about a day's journey to the west, the hill where Agric-
ola and his Romans left a camp behind them. At the foot of it I
was born, and there both father and mother still live to love me. And
so one must let Time work.

"But whither am I wandering? Let me confess to you I am uncertain about my future literary activity, and would gladly learn your

opinion concerning it; at least pray write to me again, and speedily, that I may feel myself united to you. The only piece of any importance that I have written since I came here is an 'Essay on Burns.' Perhaps you never heard of him, and yet he is a man of the most decided genius; but born in the lowest rank of peasant life, and through the entanglements of his peculiar position was at length mournfully wrecked, so that what he effected was comparatively unimportant. He died, in the middle of his career, in the year 1796. We English, especially the Scotch, loved Burns more than any poet that had lived for centuries. I have often been struck by the fact that he was born a few months before Schiller, in the year 1759, and that neither of them ever heard the other's name. They shone like stars in opposite hemispheres, or, if you will, the thick mist of earth intercepted their reciprocal light."

Goethe, commenting upon this letter, says that Burns was not unknown to him. He speaks in the highest terms of the exactness with which Carlyle had entered into the life and individuality of Schiller, and of all the German authors whom he had introduced to his countrymen. He prefaces his translation of the "Life of Schiller" with two pictures of the residence of Carlyle. In the year after the above letter was written, Mr. Carlyle wrote another letter to Goethe in reply to one from the latter, which I have not seen published in England, but is interesting as indicating the feeling in that country towards German literature up to the time at which he began his work. This letter was written on December 22, 1829, and in it Carlyle says, " You will be pleased to hear that the knowledge and appreciation of foreign, and especially of German, literature spreads

with increasing rapidity wherever the English tongue
rules; so that now at the Antipodes, in New Holland
itself, the wise men of your country utter their wisdom. I have lately heard that even in Oxford and
Cambridge, our two English universities, hitherto
looked upon as the stopping-place of our peculiar
insular conservatism, a movement in such things has
begun. Your Niebuhr has found a clever translator
at Cambridge, and at Oxford two or three Germans
have already enough employment in teaching their
language. The new light may be too strong for certain eyes, yet no one can doubt the happy consequences that shall ultimately follow therefrom. Let
nations, as individuals, only know each other, and
mutual jealousy will change to mutual helpfulness;
and instead of natural enemies, as neighboring coun-
tries too often are, we shall all be natural friends."

## VIII.

What Carlyle's parents hoped he would become—
a preacher—that he was, in a far wider way than
they could have anticipated. His casual, or even
half-cynical, remarks, bearing on religious matters,
were searching sermons. In Christmas week, he
said to his friend William Allingham that he had
observed an unusual number of drunken men in the
street, and "then," he quietly added, "I remembered
that it was the birthday of the Redeemer." Car-

lyle's very oaths were more devout than many ben-
edictions. I have heard none of the " sham damns
which disgust " (as Emerson said in his lecture on
" Superlatives "), but great sentences pronounced on
wrong with the solemnity of a foreman speaking for
an invisible jury. Being in Scotland at the house of
an old acquaintance, whom he knew to be a sceptic,
Carlyle was shocked, when dinner came, by the complaisance with which his entertainer—evidently because of the neighbors present—entered upon a sanc-
timonious " grace-before-meat " of the long Scotch
pattern ; and cut it short by exclaiming, " Oh, ——,
this is damnable !"

I believe that a careful criticism of Carlyle's style
of writing, which has puzzled so many, would show
it to be largely a scholastic exaltation and expansion
of the Dumfriesshire dialect. And when any com-
prehensive statement of his religious position is made
(if it ever is, which is doubtful), it will be found that
the " reverences " which germinated at his mother's
knee survived in him the decay of their objects and
symbols. Nay, even the old phrases were quaintly
transfigured in the speech of this heretical Cove-
nanter. He sometimes used the metaphors of Ge-
henna in consigning dogmas about the same to the
place where he thought they belonged. It was, I
believe, the great pain of his life that he could reach
no solid shore beyond the endless quicksands of ne-

gation upon which he had entered. He could not, with many of his friends, find any spiritual hope or significance in the theory of "Evolution," and his dislike of Comte's formulas repelled him from the "Church of Humanity:" albeit the Evolutionists find texts enough in his own doctrine of Force, and the "Religion of Humanity" may be equally said to have been heralded in the "Essay on Characteristics." However, in the matter of belief, here was a powerful warrior, courageous, perfectly equipped, without post to defend or battle to fight.

"To what religion do I belong?" wrote Schiller. "To none thou mightst name. And wherefore to none? Because of my religion." It was the fervor of Carlyle's religion which led him to turn away from the Scotch Church with a breaking heart: it was that which ignored each hallowed dome which for him shut out the vault of pure reason, beneath which he knelt with never-ceasing wonder and aspiration. He acknowledged that the English Church was "the apotheosis of decency," but they who looked upon its articles as the thirty-nine pillars of the universe were apt to find those pillars toppling upon them before this Samson. The sects, for him, remained to the end, each some small umbrella which its devotees imagined to be the vault of heaven. Many years ago he was persuaded by some friends in the south of England, whom he was visiting, to go to a Nonconformist chapel on Sunday. It was, I believe, for the first time in many years that he had entered either church or chapel, and was destined to be the last. "The preacher's prayer," he said, "filled me with consternation. 'O Lord, thou hast plenty of treacle up there; send a stream of it down to us!' That was about the amount of it. He did not seem in the least to know that what such as he needed was rather a stream of brimstone. But this was only the vulgar form of what I have sometimes found beneath the more refined phraseology of 'distinguished divines,' who, for the most part, know least of what they pretend to know most. What do such know of religion? of the absolute veracity, the passionate love of truth and rectitude, unspeakable horror of the reverse, which *are* Religion? How many of them are laboring to save the people from their real Satan—alcohol, which is turning millions of them into demons? The clergy are trying to make up for the vacancy left by the decay of all real Belief with theatrical displays, candles, and costumes. Everything goes to the theatre. 'Enter Christ!' That will soon be the stage-direction. But it is all another way of saying 'Exit Christ'—which states the fact more nearly. Charles I. established the English Church in order to keep his head on his shoulders. A good many support it now for the like reason, and with as little success. Undoubtedly there are some

good men in it. There is Frederic Maurice, one of
the most pious-minded men in England. He once
wrote a novel called 'Eustace Conway:' he would
like it suppressed: it is a key to him. A young man
gets into mental doubts; a priest comes and sprinkles
moonshine over him, and then all is clear! Alas,
poor Sterling! That is what happened to *him* for a
little time. He got bravely through it; but when he
did, it became painfully evident to us that he was
too fine and thin to live among us here."

Carlyle is still thought by many people to have
been severe and unsympathetic, and that this was
owing to the despairing view of the world which
he so often took. But I remember that, when our
child died many years ago (we lonely in a foreign
land), Carlyle came and sat with us; and his tenderness, his healing words, his inspiration of courage,
made the one rainbow on that black cloud. True
to his experience that in work alone could sorrow
escape from its beleaguering cares, he, with kindly
art, suggested to me a congenial literary task. Ah,
when one was in grief and pain, what a providential
heart he had! What sincerity with his wisdom,
what bountifulness with his light and heat, and su-
periority to those selfish pettinesses, small personal
aims, which too often mingle their smoke with the
fine flame of genius!

It was in speaking of our grief, and that of others,

that he said: "I still find more in Goethe about all high things than in any other. His gleams come now from a line, or even a word, or next a scrap of poetry. He did not believe in a gray-haired Sovereign seated in the heavens, but in the Supreme Laws. A loyal soul! Concerning things unknown he has spoken the best word—*Entsagung.* In thinking about immortality, we jump to selfish conclusions, and support them as if they were piety: even if we sanctify our conclusion by associating with it our departed friends and clinging affections, it is *something you want.* But nothing can be known. Goethe says—*Entsagung.* Submission! Renunciation! That is near to it. I studied the word long before I knew what he meant by it; but I know there is such a thing as rising to that state of mind, and that it is the best. Shall it be as I wish? It shall be as it *is.* So, and not otherwise. To any and every conceivable result the loyal man can and will adapt himself; face that possibility until he becomes its equal; and when any clear idea is reached, bend to that till it becomes ideal. *Entsagung* shall then mean, 'tis best even so!"

A characteristic of Carlyle was his sympathetic interest in all animal life. Often when walking in the park he would pause to observe the sparrows which, hardly getting out of the way, would pertly turn their heads and look at him as landlords might

4*

observe a suspicious character trespassing upon their estate. This seemed to amuse him much. He had always a severe anathema for vivisection, and all cruelty to animals. "Never can I forget the horror with which I once saw a living mouse put into the cage of a rattlesnake in the Zoological Gardens, to be luncheon for that reptile. The serpent fixed upon it his hard glittering eyes, and the poor little creature stood paralyzed, trembling with terror. It seemed to me a cruelty utterly unjustifiable, and one to be unceasingly protested against." The compassion of Burns for the field-mouse, whose home and hopes his plough had overthrown, was in Carlyle's tone of voice in this and much else that he said concerning his humble contemporaries of the animal world. No reader of "Sartor Resartus" can lose the image of the little boy at Ecclefechan, therein called Entepfuhl, dreaming over the migration and return of the swallows. "Why mention our Swallows, which, out of far Africa, as I learned, threading their way over seas and mountains, corporate cities and belligerent nations, yearly found themselves, with the month of May, snug lodged in our Cottage Lobby? The hospitable Father (for cleanliness' sake) had fixed a little bracket plumb under their nest: there they built, caught flies, and twittered, and bred; and all, I chiefly, loved them. Bright, nimble creatures, who taught *you* the mason-craft; nay, stranger still, gave you a masonic incorporation, almost social police? For if, by ill chance, and when time pressed, your House fell, have I not seen five neighborly Helpers appear next day, and swashing to and fro, with animated, loud, long-drawn chirpings, and activity almost super-hirundine, complete it again before nightfall?" This picture rose again before me one day when Carlyle was speaking of an experience of the philosopher Kant, when he was walking in a wood, near the wall of a ruin. He heard a clamor among the swallows, high up on the wall, so loud that it made him pause. The birds were in shrill debate about something. Presently there was a pause, then a long, low, plaintive note from one of them; and immediately thereafter a nestling, not yet able to fly, fell to the ground. Kant concluded that the debate was that of a council which decreed that there was not nest-room or food enough for all the little ones; one must be sacrificed; and the one low, plaintive note was that of the mother submitting to the fatal conclusion. Kant picked up the fallen swallow, which was not yet dead, and looked into its eye. How deep it was! As he gazed in it he seemed to be looking into an infinite depth, a mystical vista. "This struggle for existence," said Carlyle, " of which our scientific men say so much, is infinitely sad. We see it all around us. Our human reptiles are outcomes of it. Somebody told me of a subtle fellow, a small lad, who heard a poor rustic, warned to take care of his money in the crowd, say he had only a pound and meant to keep it in his mouth. Soon after the street-boy crosses the poor man's path, and sets up a cry, 'You give me my money!' A crowd having gathered, the boy explains that he had been sent by his poor mother with a sovereign to buy something, had fallen, and as the money rolled away the man had picked it up and put it in his mouth. The crowd cried 'Shame!' and he from the country had to disgorge and get home as he could. The story is credible of a boy struggling for existence in this vast abyss of greed and want. Survival of the fittest! Much that they write about it appears to me anything but desirable. I was reading lately some speculations which seemed to be fine white flour, but I presently found it was pulverized glass I had got into my mouth—no nourishment in it at all, but the reverse. What they call Evolution is no new doctrine. I can remember when Erasmus Darwin's 'Zoonomia' was still supplying subjects for discussion, and there was a debate among the students whether man were descended from an oyster or a cabbage. I believe the oyster carried the day. That the weak and incompetent pass away, while the strong and adequate prevail and continue, appears true enough in animal and in human history; but there are mysteries in life, and in the universe, not explained by that discovery. They should be approached with reverence. An irreverent mind is really a senseless mind. I have always said that I would rather have written those pages in Goethe's 'Wilhelm Meister' about the 'Three Reverences' than all the novels which have appeared in my day."

## IX.

Notwithstanding his affection for Professor Tyndall, Carlyle, in scientific matters, clung to the great masters of the past, such as Faraday, for many years his personal friend, and Franklin. He often spoke of Franklin as America's greatest man, and told good anecdotes of him; among others, one I had not heard, of his going to see a church-steeple at Streatham, near London, which had been struck by lightning. Franklin predicted that, if rebuilt in the same way, the steeple would be again struck—and that was just what happened.

The hostility which his father manifested towards all works of fiction (as "downright lies") turned, in Carlyle, to the very severe standard of veracity by which he judged all such works. He had an admiration for Charles Dickens, especially after hearing that author read some of his own works. He could, he said, hardly recall any theatrical representation he had witnessed in which the whole company had exhibited more variety of effect than came from the

play of Dickens's voice and features. Thackeray
was one of his friends during life. One evening he
pointed out to me, when we were walking, an inn
to which Thackeray once retired to escape calls and
company when he had on hand a piece of work re-
quiring special care and solitude. "I learned where
he was by his sending around to our house for a
Bible. Better work might come of the writers of
books if they knew more of this working in secret
with their Bible beside them. Some novelists of
our time appear to think that study and veracity
may be dispensed with in their art. I undertook to
read a famous novel recently, in which a personage,
a carpenter, is described as putting in the door-panel
after the rest of the door was completed. The famous novelist knew nothing at all about the making
of a door. I got no farther with that book."

On one occasion, a number of persons being present, a scholarly person (a nobleman) asked Carlyle
his opinion concerning works of imagination, of
high ability, but containing incidents not quite decorous — such books as "Tom Jones" and "Roderick Random." The main question was whether
works of such character might safely be permitted
to women. "Quite as safely as to men," said Carlyle. "If the book is really valuable in other respects, I should advise them to read such and keep
quiet about it." It is hardly to be wondered, when

the woman who lived by his side is remembered, that Carlyle made a clause in his conservatism (though a curiously cautious one) in favor of the women who were seeking medical education in Edinburgh University. While filling the office of Lord Rector, his opinion on that subject was asked by a friend there. The answer returned and privately used with good effect there, in the contest, was as follows:

"5 CHEYNE ROW, CHELSEA, *February* 9, 1871.

"DEAR SIR,—It is with reluctance that I write anything to you on this subject of Female Emancipation which is now rising to such a height, and I do it only on the strict condition that whatever I say shall be private, and nothing of it get into newspapers. The truth is, the topic, for five-and-twenty years past, especially for the last three or four, has been a mere sorrow to me, one of the most afflicting proofs of the miserable anarchy that prevails in human society, and I have avoided thinking of it, except when fairly compelled. What little has become clear to me on it, I shall now endeavor to tell you.

"In the first place, then, I have never doubted but the true and noble function of a woman in this world was, is, and forever will be, that of being a Wife and Helpmate to a worthy man, and discharging well the duties that devolve on her in consequence as mother of children and Mistress of a Household—duties high, noble, silently important as any that can fall to a human creature; duties which, if well discharged, constitute woman, in a soft, beautiful, and almost sacred way, the Queen of the World, and which, by her natural faculties, graces, strengths, and weaknesses are every way indicated as specially hers. The true destiny of a woman, therefore, is to wed a man she can love and esteem, and to lead noiselessly under his protection, with all the wisdom, grace, and heroism that is in her, the life prescribed in consequence.

"It seems, furthermore, indubitable that if a woman miss this destiny, or have renounced it, she has every right, before God and man, to take up whatever honest employment she can find open to her in the world. Probably there are several or many employments now exclusively in the hands of men for which women might be more or less fit—printing, tailoring, weaving, clerking, etc. That medicine is intrinsically not unfit for them is proved from the fact that in much more sound and earnest ages than ours, before the medical profession rose into being, they were virtually the physicians and surgeons as well as sick-nurses—all that the world had. Their form of intellect, their sympathy, their wonderful acuteness of observation, etc., seem to indicate in them peculiar qualities for dealing with disease; and evidently in certain departments (that of female disease) they have quite peculiar opportunities of being useful. My answer to your question, then, may be that two things are not doubtful to me in this matter.

"1. That Women—any woman who deliberately so determines—have a right to study medicine; and that it might be profitable and serviceable to have facilities, or at least possibilities, offered them for so doing. But—

"2. That, for obvious reasons, Female Students of Medicine ought to have, if possible, Female Teachers, or else an extremely select kind of men, and, in particular, that to have young women present among young men in anatomical classes, clinical lectures, or generally studying medicine in concert, is an incongruity of the first magnitude, and shocking to think of to every pure and modest mind.

"This is all I have to say; and I send it to you, under the condition above mentioned, as a friend for the use of friends.

"Yours sincerely,

"T. CARLYLE."

The servant who burned the "French Revolution" was in the employ of Mrs. Taylor, afterwards Mrs. Mill. "One day," said Carlyle, in relating this tragedy, "Mill rushed in, and sat there, white as a sheet, and for a time was a picture of speechless terror.

At last it came out, amid his gasps, that Mrs. Taylor, to whom he had lent the manuscript in whose preparation he had been much interested, had laid it on her study-table, when her servant-girl had found it convenient for lighting the fire; each day the volume must have been decreasing, until one day, the lady coming in, found scattered about the grate the last burnt vestiges of the most difficult piece of work I had yet accomplished. The downright agony of Mill at this catastrophe was such that for a time it required all our energies to bring him any degree of consolation; for me but one task remained in that matter: the volume was rewritten as well as I could do it, but it was never the same book."

"I used to see a good deal of Mill once, but we have silently — and I suppose inevitably — parted company. He was a beautiful person, affectionate, lucid; he had always the habit of studying out the thing that interested him, and could tell how he came by his thoughts and views. But for many years now I have not been able to travel with him on his ways, though not in the least doubtful of his own entire honesty therein. His work on 'Liberty' appears to me the most exhaustive statement of precisely that I feel to be untrue on the subject treated. But, alas! the same discrepancy has become now a familiar experience. The Irishman is now about the 'freest' man in existence; he is at liberty to sit him down on his dunghill and curse all creation; 'he clothes himself with curses as with a garment;' yet what good does he or anybody else get by it all?"

In a letter written in 1832 (see Part III.) Carlyle speaks of Mill as "one of the best, clearest-headed, and clearest-hearted young men now living in London."

John Stuart Mill always seemed to me to grow suddenly aged when Carlyle was spoken of. The nearest to painful emotion in him which I ever saw was when he made that remark, "Carlyle turned against all his friends." I did not and do not think the remark correct. When Carlyle came out with his reactionary opinions, as they were deemed, his friends became afraid of him, and nearly all stopped going to see him at the very time when they should have insisted on coming to a right understanding. Carlyle was not reserved in speaking of the change which had come over his convictions. "I used to go up stairs and down spouting the oratory of all radicals, especially the negro emancipationists. Nor have I the slightest doubt that such people have sometimes put an end to the most frightful cruelties. What worth they put into such work they reaped. But it steadily grew into my mind that of all the insanities that ever gained foothold in human minds, the wildest was that of telling masses of ignorant people that it is their business to attend to the regulation of human society. I remember when Emerson first came to see me that he had a great deal to say about Plato that was very attractive, and I began to look up Plato; but, amid the endless dialectical hair-splitting, was generally compelled to shut up the book, and say, ' How does all this concern me at all ?' But later on I have read Plato with much pleasure, finding him an elevated soul, spreading a pure atmosphere around one as he reads. And I find him there pouring his scorn on the Athenian democracy —the charming government, full of variety and disorder, dispensing equality alike to equals and unequals '—and hating that set quite as cordially as the writer of the ' Latter-Day Pamphlets' hates the like of it now; expressed in a sunny, genial way, indeed, instead of the thunder and lightning with which the pamphlet man was forced to utter it. Let Cleon, the shoemaker, make good shoes, and no man will honor him more than I. Let Cleon go about pretending to be legislator, conductor of the world, and the best thing one can do for Cleon is to remand him to his work, and, were it possible, under penalties. And I demand nothing more for Cleon or Cuffee than I should be prepared to assert concerning the momentarily successful of such who have managed to get titles and high places. In that kind, for example, his Imperial Majesty Napoleon Third— an intensified Pig, as, indeed, must some day appear."

## X.

It became clear to my own mind, after a few
months' acquaintance with Carlyle, that he had in
his mind a very palpable Utopia, one neither unlove-
ly nor unjust, whose principles, if genuinely applied,
would make ordinary Conservatives glad enough to
accept those of Mill in preference. It was part of
his view, for instance, that private proprietorship in
land should be abolished; and I well remember him
building a long discourse on English "fee," Scotch
"feu," as derived from *foi, fides,* a *trust,* and destined to be that again when Cosmos replaced Chaos.
The paper-nobility would stand small chance in
his Commonwealth. It was they mainly who usurp
the posts of highest work, for which they are incompetent, and keep the true kings, the Voltaires,
Burnses, Johnsons, in the exile of mere "talk." But
I also felt that it was by a rare felicity that Margaret Fuller spoke of him as "the Siegfried of England—great and powerful, if not quite invulnerable."
His vulnerable point was a painful longing to make
present facts square with his theory and ideal. He
could not bear to think the realization of his hope so
distant as the world said. He had lived through the
generation of bread riots, Chartism, Irish rebellions,
trade-union strikes and rattenings, and longed for a
fruitful land, with bread for all, work for all, each

laborer provided for, disciplined, regulated—a great
army of honest and competent toilers, making the
earth blossom as a rose, and at the same time dwelling peacefully in patriarchally governed homes. If
this could only be realized somewhere! Then there
reached him the tidings that in the Southern States
of America there was such a fair country. I found
him fully possessed with this idea in 1863. In his
longing that his dream should be no dream, but a
reality, he had listened to the most insubstantial rep-
resentations. An enthusiastic Southern lady had
repeatedly visited him, and found easy credence to
her story that such was the inherent vitality of
slavery, and the divine force attending it, that even
then, when the South was blockaded, and harassed
by war on every side, prosperity was springing up,
and factories appearing. Southern theorists, indeed,
there were as sincerely visionary as himself, and they
came to him personally with a wonderful scheme, by
which the South and the West Indies were to be constituted into one great nation, in which the physical
beauty of the country would only be surpassed by
the songs of the happy negroes working in their own
natural clime, untainted by any of the mad, wild
strife between labor and capital, the greed of pelf, or
the ambitions of corrupt politics. As a Southern
myself, I had another story to tell. A dream as fair
had been driven from my own heart and mind when

I was able to look beyond the peaceful homes of one or two small districts in my beloved Virginia to the actual condition of the average South, and I laid before him the facts which had expelled that dream. One or two of the simplest facts which I narrated, on a day when we walked in Hyde Park, so filled him with wrath at the injustice perpetrated that his denunciations attracted the attention of loungers in the Park. I saw before me the same man that afterwards so deeply sympathized with the wronged African Langahelele, when Bishop Colenso came over from Natal to plead for him against English oppressors—the man whose voice has helped to arrest the schemes to obtain English aid for the European slave-trader, "the unspeakable Turk."

Carlyle was always most patient when he was vigorously grappled with about his facts, perhaps from a half-consciousness that there lay his weakness, and from a natural honesty of mind. Soon after David A. Wasson had written to him that stern and dignified paper which appeared in the *Atlantic Monthly*, he asked me about Wasson, and remarked that he seemed to be "an honest, sturdy, and valiant kind of man." Subsequently I had the pleasure of introducing to him the friendly but severe critic in question, and he was very genial in conversation with his American critic.

Carlyle awakened from his dream of a beautiful

patriarchal society in the Southern States slowly, but he did awake. One day he received from the Rev. Dr. Furness, of Philadelphia, as a reply to his "Ilias in Nuce" (1863), a photograph taken of the lacerated back of a negro, with the words "Look upon this, and may God forgive your cruel jest!" He asked me about Dr. Furness, and I was able to give him an account which relieved him from the suspicion that the picture was "got up" for partisan purposes. A good many things made him, as I thought, uneasy about his position in those days. But the staggering blow, dealt with all the force of love, came from Emerson. It was early in October, 1864, that I found him reading and rereading a letter from Emerson. Long years before he had written to an American, "I hear but one voice, and that comes from Concord:" the voice had now come to him again, freighted with tenderness, but also with terrible truth. He bade me read the letter. It spoke of old friendship, conveyed kindest sympathies to Mrs. Carlyle—then an invalid—mentioned pleasantly a friend whom Carlyle had introduced, and spoke of the satisfaction with which he had read the fourth volume of "Friedrich," especially the paramount fact he drew from it that many years had not yet broken any fibre of his force; "a pure joy to me who abhor the inroads which time makes in me and my friends. To live too long is the capital misfort-

une." Then Emerson's sentences turned to fire—
fire in which love was quick as enthusiasm was burning. He said he had lately lamented that he (Carlyle)
had not visited America. It would have made it
impossible that his name should ever be cited against
the side of humanity, and would have shown him the
necessities and aspirations struggling up in the free
states, though but unsteadily articulated there. "The
battle of Humanity is at this hour in America." He
longed to enlist him with his thunderbolt on the
right side. England should hold America stanch to
her best tendency. Cannot the thoughtful minds
of England see the finger-pointings of the gods
which, above the understanding, feed the hopes and
guide the wills of men? Generals have carried to
the field the same delusions as those which had misled so many Englishmen, until corrected by experience. Every one has been wrong in his guess
except good women who never despair of the ideal
right. As for Carlyle himself, there must be some
mistake; perhaps he was experimenting on idlers,
etc. But he could not by any means be disguised
from those eyes that saw deep; they knew him better than he knew himself, perhaps, certainly better
than others knew him; and so Carlyle felt when he
read in this letter, at the close, "Keep the old kindness, which I prize above words."

"No danger but *that* will be kept," said Carlyle.

"For the rest, this letter, the first I have received from Emerson this long time, fills me with astonishment. That the cleanest mind now living—for I don't know Emerson's equal on earth for perception —should write so is quasi-miraculous. I have tried to look into the middle of things in America, and I have seen a people cutting throats indefinitely to put the negro into a position for which all experience shows him unfit. Two Southerners have just been here. One of them, I should say, has some negro blood in him, and he said, quietly, the Southerners will all die rather than submit to reunion with the North. The other, a Mr. John R. Thompson, brought me an autograph letter from Stonewall Jackson."

I knew Mr. Thompson, once editor of the *Southern Literary Messenger*, very well, and said that there could be no doubt whatever of his honor and sincerity. No one could be more sensible than I was that there were in the South many excellent people, earnest and even religious believers in the system of slavery. It had been the heaviest tragedy of my personal life when I came to feel and know that so much heart and sincerity as that amid which I grew up in Virginia were pitted against all the necessary and irresistible currents and forces of the universe. My Virginian relatives and friends, or most of them, failed to get that point of view from outside which

5

residence in free states had opened to me with personally sorrowful results, and they could not see that
the movement for emancipation in the United States
was fed from world-wide sources. They thought
me a traitor to them, I feared, though I would die
to do them any service. They regarded the aboli-
tionists as wicked, self-seeking men, and they were
certainly therein proceeding against the fact and the
truth. Was Emerson a wicked, self-seeking man? I
had known Emerson—refined, retiring, loving solitude, hating mobs—I have known him for this cause
face a wild mob; and it was along with Garrison,
Wendell Phillips, and others who had thrown away
all self-interest and all popularity, to plead for justice to the race most powerless to repay them.

Carlyle said, after a long pause, and in the gentlest
voice: "All the worth they or you have put into
this thing will return to you. You must be patient
with me when I say how it all appears to me. I
cannot help admiring the Northern people for their
determination to maintain their Union. There is
Abraham Lincoln" (taking up a photograph I had
brought); "plainly a brave, sincere kind of man,
who seemed to me crying to the country, 'Come on!'
without in the least knowing where he was leading
them, or even with quiet doubts whether he might
not be leading them to a struggle against the laws
of this universe. The Americans will probably

never believe it, but no man feels more profoundly interested and concerned for all he believes really for their good than the man who now speaks to you." On another occasion he said: "Notwithstanding all the irritation which the Americans feel towards England, America owes a great deal to England; a vast deal of English courage, wealth, literature, have gone to give America her start in the world; and I have always believed it would be paid back, with compound interest, in the steady working out to demonstration of the utter and eternal impossibility of what Europe is pursuing under the name of Democracy. The Americans are powerful, but they cannot make two men equal when the universe has determined that they are and shall be unequal. They may pursue that road, and believe they are on the way to *Je*-rusalem, but they shall find it *Ge*-henna that is finally arrived at. Nor can I doubt that an increasing number of men in America perceive this just as clearly as I do, whatever they may think of negro slavery. Many an intelligent American has told me in this room what evils their country has suffered from a vast mass of crass ignorant suffrage; and I have even come to envy America her advantage over England, inasmuch as her democratic smash-up bids fair to precede ours, with little chance of preventing it. I believe it even probable that the rule of men competent to rule—as against both sham nobility and the ignorant populace—will be first established in the United States."

He was talking in this way once when an eminent American clergyman was present, and the latter began to defend with energy the right of every man to an equal vote. "Well," said Carlyle, "I do not believe that state can last in which Jesus and Judas have equal weight in public affairs."

One evening I was trying to harmonize the positive and negative poles, i. e., to make him admit the merit of certain passages in Walt Whitman. "Ah," he said, "I cannot like him. It all seems to be, 'I'm a big man because I live in such a big country.' But I have heard of great men living in very small corners of the earth. America will, perhaps, become a great as well as a big country; but it will have to learn from the experience and age of the world. The authorities of the world have always been the aged—the Senior, Senator, Sire; I am told the Indian Sachem means the same. 'Young America' must consider that."

Carlyle was born among peasants, and knew too much of them, their ignorance and superstition, to believe that their suffrage could be trusted in government; at the same time, he had observed too much the nobility and gentry to believe that theirs was more trustworthy. The intellectual world was just entering on its phase of transcendentalism, which emphasized the idea of individual "missions:" men were, greatest and smallest, "God-sent," their tasks organic. Rulers were, like poets, born—could not be made. The prophetic vision which Carlyle had caught, amid intervals of pulpit - dulness, in Ecclefechan kirk, when Christ should be on the throne and Satan chained in the pit, survived in his mature conception of the future. Against a democracy which would give Jesus and Judas equal votes, he set an order which would place the best man on the throne, and bind down the worst. To do that, he often said, was the only meaning of progress. "Harriet Martineau, after she had come from America, used to talk about 'progress' to tediousness. It's doubtful whether there is any such thing in the sense ordinarily meant. Before one rejoices in the expansion and progress of a thing, it might be well to inquire whether it is a good thing, or the reverse, which is so flourishing."

It is notable that the heroes marked out for homage by Carlyle were chiefly from the humble rank from which he had himself sprung—Luther, Burns, Johnson, Heyne, Richter, Schiller, and others. Such was this great anti-democrat's tribute to the common people, and even the poorest. It could only have been owing to the unhappy causes already intimated that he did not add to the list of those lowly-born heroes the man who, of all his contemporaries, perhaps had the best right to be there—Abraham Lincoln.

## XI.

When the poet Longfellow called at Chelsea with an introduction from Emerson, Carlyle told him that Emerson's coming to him at Craigenputtoch was "like the visit of an angel." Emerson's letter now came, after a generation had passed, as the voice of Carlyle's good angel. Never again, after that letter (of October, 1864), did I hear Carlyle speak with his former confidence concerning the issue in America. As time went on, I could perceive an increase of attentiveness in his manner towards Americans, and he seemed to be touched by the evidence that their faith in him and love for him were in nowise shaken by anything he had said or written—not even by his "Ilias in Nuce." Among the Americans who visited him in the latter years of his life were George Ripley, Samuel Longfellow, David Wasson, Wentworth Higginson, Mr. and Mrs. Forbes, and Professor Charles Norton. Concerning each of these and others I have heard him speak in a tone which indicated a quiet revolution going on in his mind. It was a rare thing at these interviews to hear any discussion of the questions raised in Emerson's letter, though Carlyle generally "bore his testimony" against democracy. But his esteem for America and Americans steadily grew, and his eyes seemed again turning with hope to the West, as in his youth when he thought of going to dwell there.

Never can I forget the conversation between Carlyle and Bayard Taylor, when the latter visited London on his way to take his place as minister at Berlin. Several years before, Bayard had called upon Carlyle, and audaciously announced that he meant to write the Life of Goethe. The old man could not allow any such liberties to be taken with his literary hero without a challenge, and set a sort of trap for this ambitious American. " But," said he, " are there not already Lives of Goethe ? There is Blank's Life of Goethe : what fault have you to find with that ?" The tone was that Blank had exhausted the subject. Bayard immediately began showing the inadequacy and errors of Blank's book, and withal his own minute and critical knowledge of Goethe, when Carlyle broke out with a laugh, saying of the *Life* he had mentioned, "I couldn't read it through." From that moment he was cordial, and recognized the man before him. And now when Bayard was once again here, and the opportunity to achieve the great work he had undertaken seemed to be within reach, he called upon Carlyle again. We found Carlyle in the early afternoon alone, and reading. He presently remembered the previous call which the young author had made upon him, and congratulated him that he belonged to a country which preferred to be represented abroad by scholars and thinkers rather than by professional diplomatists. He at once inquired

how he was getting on with his Life of Goethe, re-
marking that such a work was needed. Bayard told
him of a number of new documents of importance
which the Germans had intrusted to him. The two
at once entered upon an interesting consultation concerning the knotty points in Goethe's history. He
referred to Bayard's translation of " Faust;" with a
good-natured smile, he said, " Yours is the twentieth
version of that book which their authors have been
kind enough to place on my shelves. You have
grappled, I see, with the second part. My belief
increasingly has been that when Goethe had got
through with his 'Faust' he found himself in possession of a vast quantity of classical and mediæval
lore, demonology and what not; it was what he
somewhere called his Walpurgis Sack, which he
might some day empty; and it all got emptied, in
his artistic way, in Part II. Such is my present
impression." At length Carlyle's brougham was announced, and he must take his customary drive; but
he was evidently sorry to give up this interview.
He entered upon an impressive monologue about
Goethe, which ended with a repetition of the first
verses of the Freemason's Song. His voice trembled
a little when he came to the lines—

> "Stars silent rest o'er us;
> Graves under us silent."

" No voice from either of those directions !" he said,

with a sigh. Then Bayard took up the strain, and in warm, earnest tones repeated the remaining verses in his perfect German. Carlyle was profoundly moved. He grasped Taylor's hand, and said, "Shall I see you again ?" The other answered that he must immediately leave England, but hoped to return before long. Carlyle passed down to his carriage, but just as he was about driving off made the driver halt, and signalled to us to come near. He said to Bayard, "I hope you will do your best at Berlin to save us from further war in Europe ;" and then, after a moment's silence, "Let us shake hands once more ; we are not likely to meet again. I wish you all success and happiness."

No man was more free from personal pride than Carlyle, or more ready to confess his error when it was proven such. In early days he had retracted his sarcasms upon Sir Robert Peel, when he found that statesman possessed of the courage to turn against his own party in order to redress a great wrong suffered by the people. He had said sharp things of Palmerston too, but when that Premier died I remember his words—" Good-bye, old friend ; I shall perhaps live, at any rate England will live, long enough to see many uglier men occupying your place !" He confessed that he had been mistaken about Frederick the Great. The freethinking monarch, and friend of Voltaire, had loomed up before

5*

him as a hero; but as that biography, which has
given to the world such a grand chapter of history,
proceeded, Frederick was found to be no worshipful
man; and he said to Varnhagen von Ense that he
had no satisfaction in writing the book—" only labor and sorrow.  What the devil had I to do with
your Friedrich?"  It is my belief that it was mainly
through his absorption in that heavy task that Carlyle was so easily misled about the struggle in
America.  But this mistake he also discovered and
confessed.  An American lady, Mrs. Charles Lowell,
whose noble son was one of those Harvard youths
that fell in the war, sent Carlyle the Harvard Memorial volume.  The old man perused this volume
with close attention, and became aware that there
had been in the Northern soldiers a spirit and purpose which he had failed to recognize.  When, at
length, Mrs. Lowell personally came to see him, he
said, as he took her hand, and even with tears, " I
doubt I have been mistaken."

Those who have regarded Carlyle as a mere wor-
shipper of force have formed a superficial judgment.
What Carlyle really worshipped was work; his motto
to the last was *Laborare est orare;* and his idea of
work was a spiritual force turning some bit of chaos
into order.  In the hard hand of toil he saw a sceptre
nobler than that of many a monarch organizing disorder.  He who could denounce Napoleon III. when

the most powerful emperor in Europe, defended Mazzini while he was the most helpless exile in Europe. He who defended Governor Eyre in the belief that he had saved Jamaica from wholesale massacre was equally resolute in his sympathy with the Zulus when he saw them assailed by English troops. He never took the side of mere success. He had no sympathy with imperialism. One of his latest public acts was to protest against the proposition to raise, in Westminster Abbey, a memorial to Prince Louis Napoleon, slain by the Zulus. While he has been popularly credited with admiration for military leaders, England has not begun a war, from the Crimean to the Afghan, in which he was not opposed to his own country.

No man was a stronger hater of tyranny. He rejoiced in the American Revolution, and also in the story of the Dutch as related by Motley—a historian of whose works he spoke very warmly indeed. "Those Dutch are a strong people. They raised their land out of a marsh, and went on for a long period of time breeding cows and making cheese, and might have gone on with their cows and cheese till doomsday. But Spain comes over and says, 'We want you to believe in St. Ignatius.' 'Very sorry,' replied the Dutch, 'but we can't.' 'God! but you *must*,' says Spain; and they went about with guns and swords to make the Dutch believe in St. Igna-

tius—never made them believe in him, but did succeed in breaking their own vertebral column forever, and raising the Dutch into a great nation."
Louis Napoleon was simply a "swindler who found
a people ready to be swindled." I thought he looked
with favor upon the new French Republic, but feared
that the people of that country were of a kind to
forget the terrible experience they had with the man
of Sedan. "They are liable to fits of depression in
which they seem driven to madness. Just now they
are in their other mood of exaltation, and the fine
qualities they possess shine out. But it is a danger-
ous experiment to suddenly break the chains of an
ignorant population."

Speaking of the "mere worship of force," which
had been attributed to him, he said: "Most of that
which people call force is but the phantasm of it,
not reverend in the slightest degree to any sane
mind. Here is some small unnoted thing silently
working, or for the most part invisibly, in which
lies the real force. Plenty of noise and show of
power around us. Men in the pulpits, platforms,
street corners, crying (as I hear it), 'Ho! all ye that
wish to be convinced of the thing that is not true,
come hither;' but the quietly _true_ thing prevails at
last. I admire Phocion there among those highly
oratorical Athenians. Demosthenes says to him,
'The Athenians will get mad, and kill you some

day.' 'Yes,' says Phocion—'*me* when they are mad, *you* when they are in their senses.' They sent Phocion to look after Philip, who was coming against them. Phocion returned and told them they could do nothing against Philip, and had better make peace with him. All the tongues began to wag and abuse him. Phocion quietly broke his staff, and cast the pieces to them. Let me be out of it altogether! Demosthenes and the orators had it their own way, and the Athenians were defeated. They then had to go to Phocion to get them out of the trouble as well as he could. I think of all this when they tell me Mr. So-and-so has made a tremendous speech. If I had my way with that eloquent man, I should say to him, 'Have you yourself done, or tried to do, any of these fine things you talk about?' '*Done?*' he would most likely have to say; 'quite the reverse. The more I say them, the less need have I to do them.' Then I would just snip a little piece of that eloquent tongue off. And the next time he made an eloquent speech, I would put to him the same question, and when the like reply came, I would snip another small piece of his tongue off. And in the end very little, most likely nothing at all, of that eloquent tongue would be left. If he could not then act, at least my fine orator could be silent. The strongest force in Europe just now—Bismarck—is the silentest. He completes the slow work of seven hundred years, but neither with tongue nor pen. Not the least service he is doing Europe, could the people give right heed to it, might be regarded his demonstration that most of the ruling men esteemed as powerful are only wind-bags. The utmost strain of their power seems to be to keep themselves one day more in their pleasurable places; that exhausts them. Mere egoism, and that of the paltry kind. It might be an adequate provision for such should a fit number of flunkeys be employed, as in the case of a high personage Voltaire tells about, to go every morning and bow to them, and say, How very great and noble your Excellency is! How much reason your Excellency has to be satisfied with Himself!"

I should remark that this was said long before Prince Bismarck was suspected of conniving with Catholic reactionists. (He used to remember that the German Chancellor's name etymologically meant the "Bishop's limit.") Since then I never heard Carlyle mention him. Carlyle might scold the Socialists, but his hatred was reserved for Jesuitism—which, however, did not mean, on his lips, simply a papal Order, but always that false Spirit arraigned in his "Latter-day Pamphlets." On an occasion when some one was denouncing Jesuitism, I remember his scrutinizing the speaker rather severely, and asking him "whereabouts he could lay his hand upon anything free from Jesuitism in what is called religion nowadays?"

## XII.

Carlyle has suffered much from having his humorous exaggerations taken, as one might say, underfoot of the letter. If the parties of progress have been misled by this kind of interpretation, still more have those been mistaken who have inferred from his anti-democratic utterances a disposition to court the aristocracy. When, in the latter years of his life, some of high rank, who had forgotten, or had never read, what he used to write about "paper-nobility," began to make much of Carlyle, his tone occasionally showed that he remembered another story of his favorite Phocion, how when the Athenian Assembly applauded, he turned to his friends and asked "what bad thing he had let slip." When the Emperor of Germany sent him the Order for Civil Merit (founded by Frederick the Great), he did not refuse it, though he did not care for, and, I believe, never acknowledged it; but, as the world knows, he would not accept the patronage at home, which might imply an admission that honest thought is to be paid in royal decorations. He had not worked for such wage, and would not receive it. When, about the time in which the German honor to the biographer of Frederick came, Queen Victoria sought an interview with him, he met her at the residence of the Dean of Westminster, and her Majesty became aware that she was in the presence of a man beyond all fictions of etiquette when he said, " Your Majesty sees that I am an old man, and, if you will allow me to be seated, I may perhaps be better able to converse." The Queen bowed assent, but she had never before conversed with one of her subjects on such terms of equality. This interview took place March 4, 1869. There were present the Duchess-Dowager of Athole (in waiting on the Queen); the Princess Louise, " decidedly a very pretty young lady, and clever too ;" Sir Charles and Lady Lyell; Mr. and Mrs. Grote; and Robert Browning; besides the Dean and Lady Augusta Stanley. Carlyle entertained the Queen with a graphic account of the antiquarian and modern associations of the region where he was born, concerning which she inquired, and of Carlisle (" Caer Lewel, about the same age as Solomon "); also with much pleasant talk of Berlin and Potsdam. He told Majesty about his grandfather's ride in old times to Glasgow, when a man worth ten thousand pounds was considered a Crœsus, when the people sang psalms and the streets were silent at 9.30 P.M.— " hard, sound, presbyterian root of what has now shot up into a hemlock-tree," to which Majesty responded with a soft, low - voiced politeness which pleased Carlyle well. He went to the interview by the underground railway, and by the same conveyance " was home before seven, and out of the adventure with no more than a headache."

When the decoration of the Grand Cross of Bath was offered and declined, the throne, the ministry, and the people heard once more from the vicinity of Ayr the brave song:

> "A prince can mak a belted knight,
>    A marquis, duke, and a' that;
> But an honest man's aboon his might—
>    Guid faith he maunna fa' that!
> For a' that, and a' that,
>    Their dignities, and a' that,
> The pith o' sense, and pride o' worth,
>    Are higher ranks than a' that."

Carlyle was sensible of a certain magnanimity in Disraeli's proffer of this honor, for he had written some severe things about the Prime-minister. The two men had never been introduced to each other. Disraeli perhaps thought that Carlyle remembered an early satire he had written upon him, which was not the case, Carlyle being always utterly free from personal resentments of that kind. Their point of nearest contact was when they were sitting together upon the late Lord Derby's commission of the National Portrait Gallery. On that occasion the portrait of Lord Brougham (he still living) was offered, and though all present felt that the acceptance of it would be a bad precedent—since politicians might utilize the gallery to advance their fame—yet all hesitated to oppose the offer save one. Carlyle rose

up and said that, "since the rest hesitated, he begged
leave to move that the Brougham picture be for the
present rejected." The motion was adopted; and
Disraeli left his seat, went round to where Carlyle
was, and stood before him for a few moments, uttering no word, but fairly beaming upon the only man
who had the courage to do that which all felt to be
right.

Disraeli's letter to Carlyle was not merely munifi-
cent—offering not only the order, but also what sum
of money might be desired to support it — but it
was expressed with the finest taste and feeling. The
order was fixed on because it had been kept more
pure than others; and "since you, like myself, are
childless," wrote the Premier, the common baronetcy
seemed less appropriate. Carlyle wrote an equally
courteous and noble reply in declining. Carlyle introduced Emerson to the English public as the singular American "who did not want to be Presi-
dent," and he must now himself be recorded as the
eccentric Briton who did not want to be decorated.
One honor Carlyle did value—the naming of a green
space in Chelsea "Carlyle Square."

On Saturday, December 4, 1875, when Carlyle completed his eightieth year, a number of his friends
and others variously representing literature united in
an address to him as follows:

TO THOMAS CARLYLE.

"*Dec.* 4, 1875.

"Sir,—We beg leave, on this interesting and memorable anniversary, to tender you the expression of our most respectful good wishes.

"Not a few of the voices which would have been dearest to you to hear to-day are silent in death. There may perhaps be some compensation in the assurance of the reverent sympathy and affectionate gratitude of many thousands of living men and women throughout the British Islands and elsewhere, who have derived delight and inspiration from the noble series of your writings, and who have noted also how powerfully the world has been influenced by your great personal example. A whole generation has elapsed since you described for us the hero as a man of letters. We congratulate you and ourselves on the spacious fulness of years which has enabled you to sustain this rare dignity among mankind in all its possible splendor and completeness. It is a matter for general rejoicing that a teacher whose genius and achievements have lent radiance to his time still dwells amidst us; and our hope is that you may yet long continue in fair health, to feel how much you are loved and honored, and to rest in the retrospect of a brave and illustrious life.

"We request you to do us the honor to accept the accompanying copy of a medal designed by Mr. J. E. Boehm, which has been struck in commemoration of the day."

The medal bears on one of its faces a medallion of Mr. Carlyle, by Mr. Boehm, and on the obverse the words—"In Commemoration. Dec. 4, 1875." Silver and bronze copies were struck for the use of the subscribers, with a few for presentation to public institutions. The copy Mr. Carlyle was requested to accept was in gold.

The inhabitants of Chelsea had for many years become familiar with Carlyle's unique figure, as he took his daily and nightly walks; and when one of his friends, under a mistake, publicly stated that he (Carlyle) had been treated with disrespect by the younger *plebs* around him, the author as publicly declared the reverse to be true. The only case of this kind which I ever heard of was one in which some fine ladies were the offenders. He stumbled and nearly fell over some obstruction in the street. The ladies, who happened to be passing, laughed. Carlyle, removing his hat, bowed low to them, and went on his way.

## XIII.

Carlyle never thoroughly enjoyed Art. Had that side of him not been repressed in early life, his last years had been happier. He had, indeed, on his walls some valuable pictures, but they were portraits, or pictures which had got there for some other reason than that they were works of art. I have never doubted that he quietly included the fine arts in the ban he placed upon rhymed poetry, and that his early bias against all such things was precisely reported in Sterling's portrait of him in "The Onyx Ring." "You," says Collins to Walsingham, "you for whose pipings and madrigals the world has smooth and favorable ears, had you the heart of a man, instead of the fancy of a conjurer, might find or make the sad hour for speaking severe truths. You might inspirit and shame men into the work of painfully building up new and graver and serener hopes, instead of lulling them into a drunken dream with wanton airs and music." Walsingham replies, " One builds cyclopean walls ; another fashions marble carvings. Each must work as he can. But remember that the cyclopean walls, though they stood indeed, and stand, became useless monuments of a dead past ; and the fox and the robber kennel among the stones. The marble carvings, which humanized their own early age, are still the delight of all humane generations." The voice of Carlyle is certainly in the rejoinder of Collins. " Ay, but those marble carvings, for those who wrought and revered them, were holy realities. Our modern poems and other tinsel-work are for us mere toys, as musical snuff-boxes or gauze flowers." He admired Shakespeare as a hero, but could hardly forgive him for not having written a history of England ; and his tone about the devotion of Goethe and Schiller to the stage was sometimes apologetic. I do not remember to have heard him speak at all of the great painters and sculptors. He was impatiently, and always, searching for realities, albeit so many of them, when found, were dry and dusty. I have heard that when he first came to London he had a prejudice even against portraits. Count d'Orsay was only able

(1839) to make his clever sketch half-surreptitiously. Much difficulty the artists had in persuading him to sit for a picture. The first to coax him in that direction was his early neighbor, Maclise—a good work of art, but evidently by an artist who knew hardly more than the rest of the world at that time (1833) the man he was delineating on canvas. Samuel Laurence, who interpreted so many good heads in America, drew a good one of Carlyle, published in the American edition of his "Miscellanies." One of the most notable pictures of him is that least known, by Madox Brown. This excellent artist designed a picture of "Work," in which he desired to introduce the Rev. Frederic D. Maurice as a working-man's friend, and Carlyle as the Prophet of Work. He had no difficulty with Maurice, but Carlyle refused to sit, and could barely be persuaded to accompany the artist to South Kensington, and stand against a rail while a photographer took the full-length which Madox Brown needed. Carlyle made a grimace, however, and said, "Can I go now?" The picture represents builders busy on the street; some fashionably dressed ladies are picking their way past the bricks and mortar; Maurice looks on meditatively, and with some sadness in his face, at this continuance of the curse, "In the sweat of thy face shalt thou eat thy bread;" while Carlyle rejoices in it, and, leaning on his cane, laughs heartily—this laugh being the outcome of the grimace which he left on the photograph. Few of his portraits are satisfactory, partly, no doubt, because of the somewhat miserable look which spread over his face whenever he was induced to sit for his portrait. However, he gradually gained a respect for the artist's work, and expressed a childlike surprise and pleasure at seeing his face emerge from the chaos of pigments. Perhaps the best picture of him as a young man was-that taken by Count d'Orsay, soon after the publication of "Sartor Resartus." A fairly satisfactory picture of him is that by Robert Tait, owned by Lady Ashburton, "An Interior at Chelsea." The portrait by G. F. Watts is too gloomy; that made by Whistler is a powerful work, but makes the author, as he sits in a rude chair, hat in hand, too much like a beggar at a church door. At request of his friend, Lady Ashburton, Carlyle sat for the sculptor, Thomas Woolner. It was a very difficult work; Carlyle was now an image of still agony, and now all fluent spirit. The sculptor said it was like trying to model a flame. He has achieved the best success in that direction of art. Woolner's bust is powerful, but the better part of Carlyle cannot be suggested in marble; granite would be a better medium. Happily, about two years before Carlyle's death, his friend Mrs. Helen Allingham was able to make sketches of him from time to time, in his own home, without interfering with his ways. In her beautiful art the last years of Carlyle are preserved; he is seen reading, smoking, conversing, meditating, and even asleep. It is to be hoped that the literary art of her husband, the poet—so long intimate with Carlyle—may some day give the world from his memory companion-pictures to these.

Carlyle had much admiration for his neighbor John Leech, and thoroughly enjoyed his cartoons in *Punch*. When that master of caricature died prematurely. of a nervous disorder, from which it was thought he might have recovered but for the organ-grinders, Carlyle, who suffered from the same fraternity, mingled with his sorrow for Leech some severe sermons against that kind of liberty which "permitted Italian foreigners to invade London, and kill John Leech, and no doubt hundreds of other nervous people, who die and make no sign." John Leech was doing his work thoroughly well, and that is the only liberty worth anything. Carlyle did not attend the theatre. I have sometimes suspected that there was in him some survival of the religious horror of theatres which prevailed at Annandale. He went to hear Charles Dickens read his works, and enjoyed that extremely. " I had no conception, before hearing Dickens read, of what capacities lie in the human face and voice. No theatre-stage could have had more players than seemed to flit about his face, and all tones were present. There was no need of any orchestra." Such enjoyments were very rare, however, as, indeed, they were poor beside the scenery of history, the heroic figures of great men, and the world drama, on which the eye of Carlyle never closed. The dramatic and other arts came within his reach too late in life. He had passed the age when he could enjoy them for beauty or turn them to use; and when the further age came, and the feebleness which the arts might have beguiled, he had no pleasure in them.

## XIV.

Carlyle's was not only an essentially religious mind, but even passionately so. His profound reverence, his ever-burning flame of devout thought, made him impatient of all such substitutes for these as dogmas and ceremonies—the lamps gone out long ago. There was a sort of divine anger that filled him whenever forced to contemplate selfishness and egotism in the guise of humility and faith.

When Emerson was on one of his earlier visits to England, large numbers of fine gentlemen whom he met desired him to introduce them to Carlyle. Some of these were crack-brained egoists, others actuated, as he saw, by curiosity, and he saved such from the catastrophes they invited by saying, mildly, "Why should you wish to have aquafortis thrown over

you?" In one case Emerson's name introduced to
him a vegetarian, with whom Carlyle went to walk.
Unfortunately, his companion expatiated too much
upon his then favorite topic, upon which Carlyle
broke out with, "There's Piccadilly; there it has
been for a hundred years, and there it will be when
you and your damned potato-gospel are dead and
forgotten." He was more patient in listening to
Miss Bacon, also introduced by Emerson, when she
tried to persuade him that Shakespeare's plays were
written by Lord Bacon. Carlyle never thought very
much of the philosopher who had been unable to
recognize such a contemporary as Kepler; and his
only reply to Miss Bacon was, "Lord Bacon could as
easily have created this planet as he could have written 'Hamlet.'" I have heard that when she had gone
he added to a letter written to his friend in Concord
the brief postscript, "Your woman's mad. T. C."
He was apt to meet a new-comer as he met Bayard
Taylor, with a challenge, but knew how to yield
gracefully when he found an able man. One evening a German philologist came, who said he had
come over to investigate "the roots of the Welsh
language." Carlyle said "if a cartload of those roots
were brought to his door, he wouldn't give sixpence
for them." But the German persisted with his talk
about roots, and in ten minutes Carlyle was absorbed
in the matter and bringing out his vast lore of old

Scotch and Gaelic words, until at length the philologist went off enriched with a "cartload" of important facts. An English Unitarian who sought to enlist him in a scheme for a New Universal Church fared badly. Carlyle never liked Unitarianism, regarding it as a competitive variety of that Coleridgean "moonshine" devised by and for those who had not the courage of their principles. "If so far, why not farther?" He preferred Quakerism, the one religion before which Voltaire bowed his head. It was often the case that Carlyle's attack was a feint; if he met with a sturdy defence, implying character, he knew how to surrender graciously. A man once came in saying he had been studying Carlyle's books, and was convinced by them that every man had some work to do in the world; he had come to ask help in trying to find out what his own work was. "Ye're a great fool," exclaimed Carlyle, "to come to me to learn what you have got to find out with your heart's blood!" A modest and forcible reply, however, cleared the way for a good conversation. With men who were making sacrifices for a cause Carlyle was not only patient, but sympathetic, even when he was opposed to their cause. On the day of Mazzini's death Carlyle talked with a good deal of feeling about him. "I remember well when he sat for the first time on the seat there, thirty-six years ago. A more beautiful person I never beheld, with his soft flashing eyes and face full of intelligence. He had great talent—certainly the only acquaintance of mine of anything like equal intellect who ever became entangled in what seemed to me hopeless visions. He was rather silent, spoke chiefly in French, though he spoke good English even then, notwithstanding a strong accent. It was plain he might have taken a high rank in literature. He wrote well, as it was—sometimes for the love of it, at others when he wanted a little money; but he never wrote what he might had he devoted himself to that kind of work. He had fine tastes, particularly in music. But he gave himself up as a martyr and sacrifice to his aims for Italy. He lived almost in squalor. His health was poor from the first; but he took no care of it. He used to smoke a great deal, and drink coffee with bread crumbled in it; but hardly gave any attention to his food. His mother used to send him money; but he gave it away. When she died, she left him as much as two hundred pounds a year—all she had; but it went to Italian beggars. His mother was the only member of his family who stuck to him. His father soon turned his back on his son. His only sister married a strict Roman Catholic, and she herself became too strict to have anything to do with him. He did see her once or twice; but the interviews were too painful to be repeated. He desired, I am told, to see her again when he was dying; but she declined. Poor Mazzini! I could not have any sympathy with many of his views and hopes. He used to come here and talk about the 'solidarity of peoples;' and when he found that I was less and less interested in such things, he had yet another attraction than myself which brought him to us. But he found that *she* also by no means entered into his opinions, and his visits became fewer. But we always esteemed him. He was a very religious soul. When I first knew him he reverenced Dante chiefly, if not exclusively. When his letters were opened at the post-office here, Mazzini became, for the first time, known to the English people. There was great indignation at an English government taking the side of the Austrian against Italian patriots; and Mazzini was much sought for, invited to dinners, and all that. But he did not want the dinners. He went to but few places. He formed an intimacy with the Ashursts which did him great good—gave him a kind of home-circle for the rest of his life in England. At last it has come to an end. I went to see him just before he left London for the last time, passed an hour, and came away feeling that I should never see him again. And so it is. The papers and people have gone blubbering away over him—the very papers and people that denounced him during life, seeing nothing of the excellence that was in

him.  They now praise him without any perception
of his defects.  Poor Mazzini!  After all, he succeeded.  He died receiving the homage of the people, and seeing Italy united, with Rome for its capital.  Well, one may be glad he has succeeded.  We
wait to see whether Italy will make anything great
out of what she has got.  We wait."

Severe as Carlyle was upon mere idlers and lion-
hunters, where there was any opportunity of assist-
ing or usefully advising any one in difficulties or
seriously desirous of doing good work, no woman's
heart could be more tender.  A young Scotchman,
James Dodds, went off to England with three shillings in his pocket; at Newcastle he became one of
a strolling company of low-comedians; after that,
tried to gain a living as schoolmaster, and failed;
next, failed as an editor; and ultimately got a place
as clerk with a solicitor near Melrose, and studied
law.  But Dodds had a good deal of talent, and was
ambitious of literary fame.  A cousin of his wrote
for him to ask advice of Carlyle, who gave it:

"It is doubtful to me," he wrote, "whether the highest conceivable success in that course might not be for your cousin an evil in place
of a blessing.  I speak advisedly in this matter.  There is no madder
section of human business now weltering under the sun than that
of periodical literature in England at this day.  The meagrest bread-
and-water wages at any honest, steady occupation, I should say, are
preferable to a young man, especially for an ambitious, excitable
young man.  I mistake much if your cousin were not wise to stick

steadfastly by his law, and what benefit it will yield him, studying, of course, in all ways to perfect and cultivate himself, but leaving all literary glory, etc., etc., to lie in the distance—an obscure possibility of the future, which he might attain, perhaps, but also would do very well without attaining. In another year, it seems, his official salary may be expected to increase to something tolerable; he has his mother and loved ones within reach; he has, or by diligence can borrow, some books worth reading; his own free heart is within him to shape into humble wisdom or mar into violent madness; God's great sky is over him, God's peaceable green earth around him; I really know not that he ought to be in haste to quit such arrangements."

James Dodds followed this advice, and became an eminent lawyer. But Carlyle followed up his first advice with friendly letters. In 1841 he writes:

"By-the-way, do you read German? It would be worth your while to learn it, and not impossible—not even difficult—even where you are, if you be resolved. These young obscure years ought to be incessantly employed in gaining knowledge of things worth knowing—especially of heroic human souls worth knowing; and you may believe me, the obscurer such years are, it is apt to be the better. Books are needed, but not yet many books; a few well read. An open, true, patient, and valiant soul is needed; that is the one thing needful."

Later on, when Mr. Dodds wished to settle in London, Carlyle was prepared to aid him:

"In this immeasurable treadmill of a place I have no time to answer letters," he says, but "if at any time a definite service can be done by answering, doubt not I shall make time for it." "Of law in London," he writes again, "I know nothing practical. I see some few lawyers in society at times, a tough, withered, wiry sort of men; but they hide their law economies, even when I question them, very much under lock and key. I understand that the labor is enormous in their profession, and the reward likewise; the successful lawyer amasses hundreds of thousands, and actually converts himself into a 'spiritual speldrin'—no blessed bargain."

Mr. Dodds, who, besides becoming a successful barrister, wrote "The Fifty Years' Struggle of the Scottish Covenanters," and other works, was for many years a valued visitor at the memorable evenings in Chelsea.

Carlyle was absolutely trusted by literary people. For this reason, if he consented to be an arbiter, his arbitration was never appealed from. No one ever suspected, or could suspect, that any personal affection or prejudice could ever make the balances waver in his hand. The letter in Part III. dated September 26, 1848, for the first time herein published, written to a gentleman whom I knew, will show the wisdom and care exhibited by Carlyle in differences of such character.

## XV.

I have often recalled the words of Carlyle, in the room at Edinburgh, concerning Craigenputtoch when he last visited it: it seemed to him a Valley of Jehoshaphat. The Valley full of graves, where Jews and Mussulmans desire to be buried because, as they suppose, that is to be the scene of the final judgment! Edgar Quinet brings his Wanderer, Ahasuerus, to the

Valley of Jehoshaphat, seeking the repose which has been forbidden him until the day of judgment. In answer to his final appeal for some herb that will cure the wound in his heart, the Valley says to Ahasuerus, "My simples cure all pains but those of a heart in which the thorn remains." Carlyle, too, was a Wanderer, and wherever he went was a small tract of that sombre Valley. He had wandered out of the fore-world of thought and feeling, and come into an age to which he did not belong. The thorn in his heart, which the solitudes of Scotland could not remove, was his utter inability to bring his intellect into any harmony with the faith and ideas of the people in that region which always held his affections. After he had come to London, where he was scandalized by the frivolous and tippling habits of so many even of the literary men, he saw the old folks and friends of Scotland in rosy tints. Again and again he went back there, but, as Mrs. Carlyle told me, the majority of them were so narrow and dogmatic that Carlyle hardly drew a peaceful breath till he got back to Chelsea. But in London he was quite as much what M. Taine named him—a Mastodon. His kingdom was extinct; and as he measured bane and blessing by that past standard, his pessimism was inevitable. In the society of London Carlyle never had any pedantry about trifles of conventionality. He told me that his stomach had never ceased to

6*

protest against the late dinner-hour, but he made his
stomach submit.  He even thought his American
friends made too much complaint of the precedence
accorded titled persons in society.  It was, he said,
traditional and not quite reasonable; but it was continued mainly because of the convenience of having
already settled, without any one being responsible
for it, a matter that might become complicated and
troublesome.  It was in far other matters than these
that Carlyle failed to find his habitat.  The spiritual
pugnacity of the burgher in him was represented by
an instinctive dislike of commonplace.  He hated
what he called *Schwärmerei*—the heaping of assent
upon assent—to an almost morbid extent.  It is even
possible that if his early antislavery and other radicalism had not become so general, some of his para-
doxical writings might never have appeared.  Masses
of men following either a Bright or a Beaconsfield
were to him equally repulsive.  One evening when
I was taking tea with him, a third who was present
expressed his joy that there was one man in England
who sat down to his own cup of tea and his own
pipe, as it were under his own vine and fig-tree, and
expressed his independent views of men and events
without even remembering whether they were the
common opinion or not.  Instantly the Scotch
burgher rose again in Carlyle, and he expatiated on
the " God-fearing men " he had known in his youth.

He was apt on such occasion to take up parables sufficiently commonplace, but dressed by him in novel costumes. "Some one was telling me in Scotland of a shepherd of the moors driving some sheep into Dumfries. All at once the bell-wether took a fancy to go another road altogether, and the rest began to follow. The shepherd ran ahead and held his staff for a bar to them, a yard from the ground; but one after the other they jumped over it. The poor fellow was spattered from head to foot with mud, and got out of it as best he could. But the sheep went on and on the same wrong way; and every one jumped at the point where the shepherd's staff had once been. When one comes to think of it, there was in that whole proceeding the light of one sheep's head!"

When she who had been the mediator between Carlyle and the world he was in, but not of, was gone, it seemed to me that his mental health first gave way. Mrs. Carlyle was more than his other self. Instinctively all who came near them accepted *her* as the head in matters relating to the visible *him*. The tailor measuring him for a coat says, "Will you have a velvet collar, ma'am?" Now suddenly this "light of his life as if gone out," he seemed to grope. His eye saw but one thing clearly—a grave. He seemed to be concentrating all of his powers of vision into that lens, as if to pierce it and catch some glimpse of

that Beyond which hitherto had baffled him.   Once
he spoke to me of the "strange experiences" he had
undergone within the few months following his
wife's death.   For a year, or nearly two, it was as if
the world had become to him a realm of shadows.
The fineness of both his memory and his judgment
seemed blunted, and many of the persons he had
known, and used to describe with interest and dis-
crimination, were, if mentioned, brushed away like
flies—mere annoyance to a heart trying to find silence and repose in the grave where it lay with his
lost treasure.   After a few years he rallied from this
condition somewhat, but he was never quite the same
man again, unless in exceptional hours.   "Emerson
complains of his memory," he once said, "but I fancy
his memory is good enough; probably it is with him
as with me, much that he hears possesses no interest
for him, and comes in one ear to go out of the other."
He increasingly disliked to be in large companies,
and if any argument was begun with him was apt to
end it abruptly with a *concessum sit*.   He was restless too.

The last time that Carlyle appeared in any public
assembly was on March 5, 1879, when he went with
Allingham to hear his friend, the charming story-
teller W. R. S. Ralston, recite and interpret his fairy-
lore in St. James's Hall.   It was for the benefit of
the innocent sufferers by the failure of the City of

Glasgow Bank, with whom Carlyle sympathized. During the recital of one of the fables, a figure introduced of a Vampire seemed to him to mean all-devouring Time — *Tempus edax rerum* — and Mr. Ralston tells me that he heard Carlyle whisper that to some one beside him. Carlyle did not stay long, for already the spirit of unrest was upon him. But this story (" The Witch and the Sun's Sister," which is contained in Ralston's " Russian Folk-tales ") made an impression on him. In the tale, Prince Ivan leaves his home, being warned that his about-to-be-born sister will be a vampire, and will devour all her family. He finds two aged sewing-women, and begs to live with them; but they refuse, having no time to attend to him, since they must die as soon as they have used up a trunkful of needles. He journeys on and makes the same request of the giant Vertodub (Tree-extractor), who is also too busy, since he will have to die when he has uprooted the surrounding forests. The same happens with a further giant, Vertogon (Mountain-leveller), who is to die when he has levelled all the neighboring mountains. Ivan presses forward till he reaches the house of the sister of the Sun. He leaves her to see his old home again. She gives him a brush which produces forests, a comb which produces mountains; so on his way back Ivan gives the giants plenty of work to do, so extending their lives. He also has some talisman

which makes the old sewing-women young again.
Arrived home, he is pursued by his vampire sister;
but the giants impede her with forests and mountains, and at last he is secure in the chamber of the
Sun's sister. "None of them," said Carlyle, "could
help Ivan; they had to stick to their needles and
forest-clearings; Ivan must go on his way with the
like steadfastness and accomplish what is before him.
When he has reached the light, he can give them all
more life and work, and make their old hearts young
again at it; and, doing that, he gets beyond reach of
the Devourer."

But Carlyle himself was never an Ivan. He was
rather the giant laboring at forest and mountain to
whom no Prince from the chamber of the Sun returned. He stood faithfully to what seemed to him
his task; from it he never swerved at the call of any
passing wanderer, prince or peasant, till his hand was
palsied and his eye grew dim. Then he sighed for
Death, which was over-long in coming.

PART II.

BY THE GRAVE OF CARLYLE

# BY THE GRAVE OF CARLYLE.

Ecclefechan, *February* 10, 1881.

On Saturday last a child came to me and said, "He is dead." I did not ask, Who? For nearly two weeks all eyes in Europe and America which know the value of a great man in this world had been centred on that home in Chelsea where Carlyle lay dying. He had long been sighing for death, for, he said, "Life is a burden when the strength has gone out of it." For a long time he had been unable to receive his friends in the evening: those true Noctes Ambrosianæ were forever past. Brief interviews with intimate friends in the early afternoon, followed by a drive with one or another of them, continued for about a year more. But these drives were not cheerful. The old man's voice was sometimes scarcely audible. "The daughters of song are low." I found it painful to have to bend so close to catch the words, which when caught showed the intellect still abiding in its strength. It was long ere it must also be said, "Those that look out of the

windows be darkened." But slowly that time came
too. The old man sank into a state of painless pros-
tration. The effort to attend to what was said to
him was a disturbance, and all was silent around
him. He was conscious nearly unto the last, and
thoughtfully intimated to his nephew and niece, who
had so long watched beside him, that he was in no
pain. His last word was a gentle "Good-bye." At
half-past eight, February 5, the end came without
struggle. The golden lamp was not shattered; it
went out. And how dark seemed London that day!

On Monday morning I started northward through
a snow-storm, and in the evening was driving through
the narrow streets of Annan. Along these same
streets he and Irving used to walk in their school-
days. Next morning I called on his sister, Mrs.
Austin, who much resembles him. She spoke sweetly of her great brother in his early youth—how loving he was as a son, how affectionate to them all,
even in those days when his mind was harassed with
doubts and misgivings about the path on which he
should enter. Sleep might fail him, and appetite,
but love for those who needed his love never failed
him. She is one of two sisters surviving. The one
remaining brother, James, resides in a pleasant home
in the neighborhood, and is about seventy-five years
of age. The other surviving sister is Mrs. Aitken,
of Dumfries.

ROOM IN WHICH CARLYLE WAS BORN.

The house in which Carlyle was born will probably be preserved as a monument—perhaps with a library in it for the neighborhood. There could be none better. In this small house his parents, at his birth, were only able to occupy two rooms. That in which the great man was born is humble enough, lit by one little window—the bed built into the wall. The rooms are now occupied by the sexton who dug his grave.

Between that small room where Carlyle first saw the light, and that smaller grave which hides him from the light, it is hardly a hundred steps: yet what a life-pilgrimage lies between those terms! what stretches of noble years, of immense labors, of invincible days rising from weary nights, mark the fourscore years and five that led from the stone-mason's threshold to a hero's tomb!

What could his parents give him? An ever-present sense of an invisible world, of which this life is the threshold—a world of transcendent joys marking the crown which the universe prepares for virtue, with an underside of unspeakable pains which mark the eternal brand fixed on evil-doing. Of this world they could teach him little, only that it was a place of brief probation by suffering and self-denial. For the rest they can only send him to a poor little school hard by. It, and Ecclefechan influences generally, are travestied in the experiences of Herr Teufels-

dröckh in his native "Entepfuhl." "Of the insignificant portion of my education which depended on
schools," he says, "there need almost no notice be
taken. I learned what others learn, and kept stored
by in a corner of my head, seeing as yet no manner
of use in it."

But, meanwhile, there is another university than
that at Edinburgh, and little Thomas is already studying in it more deeply than pedagogue or parent sus-
pects. That university is the universe itself, and
little by little he finds that Ecclefechan is a centre
of it. The little burn runs before the door; as he
wades in it the brook whispers of its course as it
passes on to the river, on to the sea, out into the
universe. The swallows come from afar — from
Africa and other regions—to nestle in the eaves of
the house. The stage-coach, as it comes and departs,
becomes mystical to the lad when he learns that it
connects the village with distant cities, and is weaving human habitations together like a shuttle. The
village road leads to the end of the world.

On the day before the funeral I went out to
Craigenputtoch, the name of the solitude in whose
one house Carlyle and his wife began life together.
The nearest railway-station is about ten miles distant from the place, and, as I was warned, affords no
means of conveyance, so I started in a carriage to
drive over the fifteen miles of country road. It is

CRAIGENPUTTOCH.

a pilgrimage not without way - side shrines. Dumfries, to begin with, is the town of Robert Burns, who died July 21, 1796, when Carlyle was in his eighth month. Here, in the church - yard, is the beautiful monument of Burns: the Muse touches him on the shoulder as he holds the plough. On the outward road we pause at Iron Gray Church to see the tomb which Sir Walter Scott erected over Helen Walker, whom he had made the friend and exemplar of many children under the name of Jeannie Deans, the girl who would not swerve from verbal truth to save her sister's life, but did journey to London on foot to save her. The epitaph bids the wayfarer "Respect the grave of poverty when combined with love of truth and dear affection." Not much farther on is the solitary monument of the old decipherer of mossy epitaphs, "Old Mortality." Now and then a stately old mansion is passed, and some cultured vales, but at length the road enters upon a wild, bleak country. The snow covers the desolate moors; the road is stony; but it is all picturesque as I remember how along every mile of it Emerson drove in a gig to clasp heart and hand of his young intellectual brother forty - eight years before. " I found the house amid desolate heathery hills, where the lonely scholar nourished his mighty heart." And now, too, I found it, the home of a kindly shepherd and his family. Arthur Johnstone-Douglas, of Glen

Stuart, is with me, and we are given by the humble people welcome and refreshment. We sit in the room where "Sartor Resartus" was written. Here gathered around the young thinker the faces of the great with whom he spiritually conversed, "never less alone than when alone." Here were written many of those essays which, as Emerson said when collecting them, had deprived their readers of sleep.

The house itself is much the same in appearance as it was when Goethe had a sketch of it made for his translation of Carlyle's "Life of Schiller." A large kitchen was added at a later period, and several out-houses. There are about a thousand acres of the estate, though much of it is uncultivated. While Carlyle resided there he was only able to cultivate some two hundred acres, most of the produce of which went in the shape of rental to the widow Welsh, Mrs. Carlyle's mother. Only at her death did it come into the possession of Carlyle's wife. Up to the present time it had belonged to the author, and has been under the care of his brother James, and his son of the same name. It would now revert to the Welsh family, were any representative of it living; as it is, Craigenputtoch will become the possession of Edinburgh University. The house is neat and comfortable. The room which was used for a library is commodious, though the out-looks are sombre enough. However, there are fine

MRS. THOMAS CARLYLE.

old ash-trees around, and near-by there was in those days a noble grove to make up for the treeless barrenness of the surrounding landscape.

But no place could be joyless where Jane Welsh Carlyle was. I have just seen a portrait of her, taken when she was young. No one who saw her only in the days of her invalidism can imagine how bright and beautiful she then was. The face is full of mirth and graciousness, refined and spirituelle. One can imagine that graceful form moving daintily amid the wood and heather, and the merry laugh that made the solitude gay.

The solitude was not unvisited by a certain class of guests. "Poor Irish folk come wandering over these moors," he said to Emerson. "My dame makes it a rule to give every son of Adam bread to eat, and supplies his wants to the next house. But here are thousands of acres which might give them all meat, and nobody to bid these poor Irish go to the moor and till it. They burned the stacks, and so found a way to force rich people to attend to them." When Carlyle died, the Irish were again burning stacks, and the rich attending to them.

For the rest, there was "not a person to speak to within sixteen miles, except the minister of Dunscore." Yet Carlyle's heart was still clinging to his kindred in the far-away people among whom he was born. In 1832 he heard that the cholera was devastating Dumfries.   He wrote the following letter to his mother's brother, addressed to " Mr. John Aitken, mason, Friars' Vennel, Dumfries :"

"CRAIGENPUTTOCH, *October* 16, 1832.

"MY DEAR UNCLE,—Judge if I am anxious to hear from you. Except the silence of the newspapers, I have no evidence that you are still spared.   The disease, I see, has been in your street; in Shaw's; in Jamie Aitken's; it has killed your friend Thomson : who knows what further was its appointed work?   You I strive to figure in the meanwhile as looking at it, in the universal terror, with some calmness, as knowing and practically believing that your days and the days of those dear to you were now, as before and always, in the hand of God only, *from* whom it is vain to fly, *towards* whom lies the only refuge of man.   Death's thousand doors have ever stood open; this, indeed, is a wide one, yet it leads no farther than they all lead.

" Our boy was in the town a fortnight ago (for I believe, by experience, the infectious influence to be trifling, and quite inscrutable to man, therefore go and send whithersoever I have *business*, in spite of cholera); but I had forgot that he would not naturally see Shaw or some of you, and gave him no letter, so got no tidings.   He will call on you to-morrow, and in any case bring a verbal message.   If you are too hurried to *write* in time for him, send a letter next day ' to the care of Mrs. Welsh, Templand, Thornhill ;' tell me only that you are all spared alive.

" We are for Annandale after Thornhill, and may possibly enough return by Dumfries.   I do not participate in the panic.   We were close beside cholera for many weeks in London.   ' Every ball has its billet.'

" I hear the disease is fast abating.   It is likely enough to come and go among us, to take up its dwelling with us among our other maladies.   The sooner we grow to compose ourselves beside it, the wiser for us.   Man who has reconciled himself *to die* need not go distracted at the *manner* of his death.

"God make us all ready, and be his time ours! No more to-
night.

"Ever your affectionate      T. CARLYLE."

Hither Emerson's divining-rod brought him in
1833. "Straight uprose that lone wayfaring man,"
to commune with one lonelier than himself, while as
yet but few had heard the names of either. On leaving Craigenputtoch, we passed a craggy brow, high
on the left, overlooking Dunscore, which was easily
identified as the point where Carlyle and Emerson
sat together. "There we sat down," wrote Emerson,
"and talked of the immortality of the soul." There
Carlyle said, "Christ died on the tree: that built
Dunscore kirk yonder; that brought you and me
together. Time has only a relative existence."

The last words Carlyle ever said to me were,
"Give my love to Emerson. I still think of his visit
to us in Craigenputtoch as the most beautiful thing
in my experience there."

That high point, where the two young thinkers sat
and conversed, appeared to me as a latter-day Pisgah:
only one of them was to enter the Land of Promise
they beheld from afar. One returned to his Valley
of Jehoshaphat to dwell with the shades of heroes
whose world is forever past; the other passed on to
greet the heralds of a world unborn. Despair and
Hope have found their fullest utterances in the Old-
World scholar and the New-World prophet who met

7

and parted on that lonely height of Scotland forty-eight years ago.

Dunscore village is seven miles from Craigenputtoch. The shepherd told us that the minister there was very aged, and had been there a long time; probably would have known Carlyle. So we drove over to Dunscore, and visited the Manse, as the parsonage is termed in Scotland. The aged minister said he had come there after Mr. Carlyle had gone to London; he had never seen him. "But he was one of my *heritors*" (i. e., pecuniary helpers), "and my acquaintance with him was limited to correspondence concerning the educational needs of this district, in which I am bound to say he liberally assisted."

The funeral of Carlyle, it may be assumed in accordance with his expressed wishes, was singularly private. Neither the day nor the place of it was known to the public. It was generally supposed that he would be buried beside his wife amid the mouldering walls of Haddington Cathedral. How strong were the ties that bound his heart to that spot is shown in the tribute on her grave. But with so much else which Carlyle had derived from his early Hebrew training, he had a desire, like that of the patriarchs, to be "gathered to his people." But for his love of his people, lowly as they were, probably the grave of Carlyle would have been in America. "I have," he said to Edward Irving, when they were young men together—"I have the ends of my thoughts to bring together, which no one can do in this thoughtless scene. I have my views of life to reform, and the whole plan of my conduct to re-model; and withal I have my health to recover. And then once more I shall venture my bark upon the waters of this wide realm, and, if she cannot weather it, I shall steer west and try the waters of another world." This alternative must have recur-red to him when America alone was listening to his voice; when his spiritual biography, in "Sartor Re-sartus," unpublished in England, was already speak-ing to American youth, as Emerson said, with an em-phasis that deprived them of sleep. But Carlyle loved his widowed mother and his people, and could not leave them. And his last wish was to rest among them. As Israel died in an Egyptian palace, and would have been laid by Pharaoh in the proudest pyramid, but charged his sons, "Ye shall bury me with my people," so could not Carlyle rest in West-minster Abbey, which was offered, nor in Hadding-ton Cathedral, where his wife's wealthier kindred lay. Ecclefechan, long raised from obscurity by be-ing his birthplace, is now consecrated by holding his dust.

Had Carlyle's aversion to all pomp and ostenta-tion not caused such strict privacy to be observed, the funeral would have been one of vast dimensions.

The Scotch gentry would have stood beside the
grave of one of whom they were proud; but as it
was, a red-coated fox-hunt was going on in the
neighborhood.  A new minister, too, was installed
that day in the neighboring kirk of Cummertrees.
As I drove to the funeral I met the more well-to-do
folk of Ecclefechan driving thither.  Those left in
the village seemed to be mainly peasants and their
children.  These were made aware of the hour when
the burial was to take place by the tolling of the
bell in the School Board building.  Hundreds of
children gathered near the gate of the church-yard
or climbed on the walls.  About a hundred young
workmen made their way inside, and stood awaiting the arrival of the body after the night journey
from London.  Soon after noon the hearse drove
up; with it five coaches, containing the relatives.
The coffin was of plain oak.  On it was engraved,
"Thomas Carlyle: born December 4, 1795; died
February 5, 1881."  White flowers were upon it,
among them a large wreath.  Along with the male
relations stood a very few personal friends of Carlyle, foremost among them Anthony Froude, Professor Tyndall, and Mr. Lecky.  With exception of
these, and a few journalists, they who gathered
around Carlyle's grave were of the peasantry.

What did these lowly ones think as they saw their
great villager laid to rest?  It was amid profound

stillness: there was no ceremony; no word broke
that silence amid which the prophet of Silence was
laid to rest. But those young workmen may have
heard still, small voices. One of these might have
come from the family tomb, which bears this in-
scription:

"Erected to the memory of Jannet Carlyle, spouse
to James Carlyle, mason in Ecclefechan, who died
the 11th September, 1792, in the twenty-fifth year
of her age. Also Jannet Carlyle, daughter to James
Carlyle and Margaret Aitken: she died at Ecclefechan, January 27, 1801, aged seventeen months.
Also Margaret their daughter: she died June 22,
1830, aged twenty-seven. And the above James
Carlyle, born at Brownknowe in August, 1758, died
at Scotsbrig on the 23d January, 1832, and now also
rests here. And here also now rests the above Margaret Aitken, his second wife: born at Whitestanes,
Kirkmahoe, in September, 1771; died at Scotsbrig
on Christmas-day, 1853. She brought him nine
children, whereof four sons and three daughters survived, gratefully reverent of such a father and such
a mother."

The last sentence was added by Thomas Carlyle.
It is almost the only touch of feeling discoverable in
the crowded church-yard. Some of the old slabs
are carved with skull and cross-bones, but their inscriptions are merely names and dates. Some of the

old folk of this region are still in the cross-bone stratum of belief. "What a pity yon man Tom Caerl was an infidel!" one was heard saying to another along the road. The two shook their heads over their greatest countryman. What notions they had of fidelity who regarded that life as product of infidelity were an antiquarian speculation. The younger peasantry of Ecclefechan, reading that tribute on the tomb, seeing the great man laid beside his lowly parents, bringing there whatever lustre surrounded his name, will probably reflect that a man may depart from the creed and the ways of his people, might become famous enough to refuse decorations proffered by royalty, yet preserve the simplicity and the affections of his early life. They may have been impressed, in that silence, by the fact that here was one of themselves—nay, as the tolling School Board bell might remind them, with less advantages than theirs—who climbed upward, and gained the love and honor of the world.

It is said that the name of this village means the Ecclesia of St. Fechan, and that the ancient church stood near the spot where Hoddam kirk now stands. Beside this church stood the school to which Carlyle was sent as a child. There taught the poor "down-bent, broken-hearted, under-foot martyr," the teacher who "did little for me except discover that he could do little." At any rate, the poor man pronounced

Thomas a genius, fit for a learned profession. In looking after the site of the old school-house, I found at Hoddam an old man who had been a pupil there with Thomas. He was aged and shivering as he moved slowly amid the snow. He said, "Tom always sent me something every year—until this last winter; then it stopped."

Then it stopped! And how much has stopped besides this poor brother's little winter solace! What charities to hearts and minds in their sore need, what brave words of cheer for those moving about in worlds not realized! Graduation from "Carlyle Close," now a shamble, to the highest intellectual distinction of the nineteenth century implies the realization of several worlds dim to others. Out of a depth like this his voice will always go forth, and to it the deeps will always answer. The influence of Carlyle will never "stop:" wherever shams are falling, his sturdy blows will still be heard; generations of the free will recognize that they are offspring of the fire in his heart, burning all fetters; and when the morning stars sing together of dawning days, when heroes of humanity replace nobles without nobility and bauble-crowned kings, his voice, so long a burden of pain, will be heard again rising into song.

THOMAS CARLYLE.

# PART III

# LETTERS OF CARLYLE

(WITH ONE FROM EMERSON)

# EXPLANATORY NOTE.

THE following extracts, from early letters of Thomas Carlyle, require a few words of explanation:

In the year 1838 a friend kindly lent me for perusal a bundle of letters, numbering between forty and fifty, written by Thomas Carlyle, addressed to two intimate and evidently much-beloved college friends. The earliest date of these letters was 1814, when the writer of them was nineteen years of age, and the latest 1824, the year in which he first visited London. These two friends were Thomas Mitchell, afterwards one of the classical masters in the Edinburgh Academy, who died before 1838, and Thomas Murray, afterwards Dr. Thomas Murray, author of "The Literary History of Galloway," a lecturer, in later years, on political economy, and subsequently partner in a printing firm in Edinburgh. He also is dead.

At the time when these letters were lent to me I had just been reading with absorbing interest and

admiration that marvellous book—the book of the
century—"The French Revolution; a History," by
Thomas Carlyle, which produced a deeper and more
vivid impression on my mind than any work I had
ever met with before. His early articles in the
*Edinburgh* and other reviews were familiar to me,
and in 1837 I had received from Mr. Emerson a
copy of the first edition, published at Boston, United
States, of "Sartor Resartus," reprinted from *Fraser's Magazine* (prior to any reprint in this country).
To me, therefore, the privilege of reading this batch
of letters was a treat of no common kind. With
eager delight I commenced their perusal at a late
hour, and never ceased until I had finished them in
the early hours of morning. In these letters Carlyle poured out to his two college-mates his inmost
thoughts and feelings with unstinted frankness. He
confided to them his aspirations, his failures, his
glooms and despondencies, his struggles, hopes, and
disappointments, while bravely battling with hard
fortune and uncongenial work, and as yet unable to
find his true vocation. There are passages in these
letters which I venture to say are not surpassed by
anything he has since written; and many of them
afford a deeply interesting insight into his mind and
character. So much was I struck with this that I
ventured to make copious extracts, sitting up through
the best part of a couple of nights for this purpose.

When I restored the precious packet to the kind friend who had lent it, I was asked whether I had made any transcripts. While confessing my transgression, if transgression it could be called, I was allowed to retain what I had copied on the distinct understanding that during Carlyle's lifetime not a line should be allowed to get into print. This pledge I have strictly kept. A few years ago the matter was mentioned to the venerable writer of the letters by a common friend. His deliverance on the matter was—a hearty laugh, accompanied with an expression of surprise, not unmingled with satisfaction, that there was any one, at that early time, who felt so much interest in him and his doings as to have taken the trouble to preserve these records of his youthful thoughts and feelings and struggles.

In conclusion, let me say that I thought it due to Mr. Froude to submit these extracts to him, and to place them at his disposal for use in the forthcoming "Life and Letters" from his pen, in case the original letters themselves should not come into his possession—at the same time asking to be allowed to make them public, in the event of his not being able to use the whole of them, from the abundance of material likely to be in his hands. I need not say that I should regret the withholding of a single sentence of these extracts, they are so characteristic throughout.   Mr. Froude has been so kind as to say that there can be no objection to their publication, as it is most desirable that the fullest light should be thrown on every period of Carlyle's life.

ALEXANDER IRELAND.

INGLEWOOD, Bowdon, Cheshire, *April 14th*, 1881.

# LETTERS OF THOMAS CARLYLE.

**1.**

*"August,* 1814.

"But—O Tom! what a foolish, flattering creature thou art! To talk of future eminence in connection with the literary history of the nineteenth century to such a one as me! Alas! my good lad, when I and all my fancies and reveries and speculations shall have been swept over with the besom of oblivion, the literary history of no century will feel itself the worse. Yet think not, because I talk thus, I am careless about literary fame. No, Heaven knows that ever since I have been able to form a wish, the wish of being known has been the foremost. O Fortune! thou that givest unto each his portion in this dirty planet, bestow (if it shall please thee), coronets and crowns, and principalities and purses, and pudding and power upon the great and noble and fat ones of the earth; grant me that, with a heart of independence, unyielding to thy favors and unbending to thy frowns, I may attain to literary fame—and, though starvation be my lot, I will smile that I have not been born a king ! ! !　But, alas! my dear Murray, what am I, or what are you, or what is any other poor unfriended stripling in the ranks of learning?

"'Ah, who can tell how hard it is to climb,' etc., etc.

\*　　\*　　\*　　\*　　\*　　\*

"The more I know her and her species, the more heartily I despise them.　It is strange, but it is true, that by a continued and unvarying exercise of affectation, those creatures in the end entirely lose any kind of real feeling which they might originally have possessed.　Ignorant, formal, conceited, their whole life is that of an *automaton*, without sense, and almost without soul!　Once, for instance, I recollect that to fill up one of those awful *hiatus* in conversation that occur at times in spite of all one's efforts to the contrary, and to entertain Miss M——, I took up a 'Tristram Shandy,' and read her one of the very best jokes within the boards of the book. Ah-h-h-h! sighed Miss M——, and put on a look of right *tender melancholy!*　Now, did the smallest glimmering of reason appear here?　But I have already wasted too much time on her and those like her.　Heaven be their comforter!

"I regret that Jeffrey should bestow so much of his time upon politics, and I rejoice in the prospect (for this is one of the advantages of Peace) that in a short time he will not have this in his power.　He must be an extraordinary man. No subject, however hackneyed, but he has the wit of extracting some new thought out of it. The introduction to the criticism on Byron is, in my opinion, admirable—so acute, so philosophical; none but a man of keen penetration and deep research could have written such a thing. Even the 'Present State of Europe' becomes interesting in his hands."

2.

"*April*, 1815.

"But the book I am most pleased with is 'Cicero de Finibus'—not that there is much new discussion in it, but his manner is so easy and elegant; and, besides, there is such a charm connected with attending to the feelings and principles of a man over whom 'the tide of years has rolled.' We are entertained even with a common sentiment; and when we meet with a truth which we ourselves had previously discovered, we are delighted with the idea that *our* minds are similar to that of the venerable Roman."

3.

"ANNAN, *June* 21, 1815.

"The most disagreeable circumstance in a tutor's life is his want of society. There is no person in the family of equal rank with him except the governess; and as the aims and ends of her and him are often various, and their dispositions heterogeneous, the tutor is, for the most part, left to commune with himself. Such a situation, in this view, is not desirable; but the power of habit is unlimited, and, at any rate, this state has its advantages: the increase of opportunities it affords for study are obvious; and though we cannot enjoy the spirit-stirring *crack* of our jocund cronies, yet if we can spend the same time with Shakespeare or Addison, or Stewart, we are gainers by the privation. I grant we cannot always live with your sages and your demigods; but no conversation at all is preferable to the gossiping and tittle-tattle that many a poor wight is forced to brook,—e. g., your humble servant,—living 'Pelican in the Wilderness' to avoid the cant and slang of the coxcombs, the bloods, the bucks, the boobies, with which all earth is filled."

### 4.

"ANNAN, *August* 22, 1815.

" * * * His (Lord Kaimes's) works are generally all an awkward compound of ingenuity and absurdity, and in this volume ["Essays on the Principles of Morality"] the latter quality, it appears to me, considerably preponderates. It is metaphysical—upon Belief, Identity, Necessity, etc. I devoutly wish that no friend of mine may ever come to study it, unless he wish to learn

" 'To weave fine cobwebs, fit for skull
That's empty, when the moon is full;'

and in that case he cannot study under a more proper master. * * * [I am] becoming daily more lukewarm about the preaching business."

5.

"ANNAN, *December 5,* 1815.

"* * * I had a sight of 'Waverley' soon after I received your letter, and I cannot help saying that, in my opinion, it is by far the best novel that has been written these thirty years—at least, that I know of. Eben. Cruickshanks, mine host of The Seven Golden Candlesticks, and Mr. Gifted Gilfillan, are described in the spirit of Smollett or Cervantes. Who does not shed a tear for the ardent Vich Ian Vohr, and the unshaken Evan Dhu, when, perishing amid the shouts of an English mob, they refuse to swerve from their principles? And who will refuse to pity the marble Callum Beg, when, hushed in the strife of death, he finishes his earthly career on Clifton Moor, far from the blue mountains of the North, without one friend to close his eyes? 'Tis an admirable performance. Is Scott still the reputed author?"

[In this letter Carlyle mentions reading Euler's "Algebra," Addison's "Freeholder," Cuvier's "Theory of the Earth," Molière's "Comedies," the monthly reviews, critical journals, etc.]

### 6.

"*February* 20, 1818.

"After an arduous struggle with sundry historians of great and small renown, I sit down to answer the much-valued epistle of my friend. Doubtless you are disposed to grumble that I have been so long in doing so; but I have an argument in store for you. To state the proposition logically: This letter, I conceive, must either amuse you or not. If it amuse you, then certainly you cannot be so unreasonable as to cavil at a little harmless delay; and if it do not, you will rejoice that your punishment has not been sooner inflicted. Having thus briefly fixed you between the horns of my dilemma, from which, I flatter myself, no skill will suffice to extricate you, I proceed with a peaceful and fearless mind.

"* * * I continue to teach (that I may subsist thereby), with about as much satisfaction as I should beat hemp, if such were my vocation. Excepting one or two individuals, I have little society that I value very highly; but books are a ready and effectual resource. May blessings be upon the head of Cadmus, or the Phœnician, or whoever it was that invented books! I may not detain you with the praises of an art that carries the voice of man to the extremities of the earth, and to the latest generations; but it is lawful for the solitary wight to ex-

press the love he feels for those companions so steadfast and unpresuming, that go or come without reluctance, and that, when his fellow-animals are proud
or stupid or peevish, are ever ready to cheer the lan-
guor of his soul, and gild the barrenness of life with
the treasures of bygone times. Now and then I
cross the Firth ; but these expeditions are not attended with much enjoyment. The time has been when
I would have stood a-tiptoe at the name of Edinburgh ; but all that is altered now. The men with
whom I meet are mostly preachers and students in
divinity. These persons desire not to understand
Newton's Philosophy, but to obtain a well-plenished
manse. Their ideas, which are uttered with much
vain jangling, and generally couched in a recurring
series of quips and most slender puns, are nearly con-
fined to the Church, or rather Kirk-session politics
of the place ; the secret habits, freaks, or adventures
of the clergy or professors ; the vacant parishes and
their presentees, with patrons, tutors, and all other
appurtenances of the tithe-pigtail. Such talk is very
edifying certainly ; but I take little delight in it.
My theological propensities may be included within
small compass ; and with regard to witlings, gibers,
or such small gear, the less one knows of them it is
not the worse.

"My perusal of Smollet's 'Continuation' was a
much harder and more unprofitable task. Next I

read Gibbon's 'Decline and Fall,' a work of immense research and splendid execution. Embracing almost all the civilized world, and extending from the time of Trajan to the taking of Constantinople by Mahomet II., in 1453, it connects the events of ancient with those of modern history. Alternately delighted and offended by the gorgeous coloring with which his fancy invests the rude and scanty materials of his narrative, sometimes fatigued by the learning of his notes, occasionally amused by their liveliness, frequently disgusted by their obscenity, and admiring or deploring the bitterness of his skilful irony, I toiled through his many tomes with exemplary patience. His style is exuberant, sonorous, and epigrammatic to a degree that is often displeasing. He yields to Hume in elegance and distinctness, to Robertson in talent for general disquisition; but he excels them both in a species of brief shrewd remark for which he seems to have taken Tacitus as a model, more than any other that I know of. The whole historical triumvirate is abundantly destitute of virtuous feeling, or indeed of any feeling at all. I wonder what benefit is derived from reading all this stuff. What business of mine is it though Timur Bey erected a pyramid of 80,000 human skulls in the valley of Bagdad, and made an iron cage for Bajazet? or what have I to do with the cold-blooded savage policy of [illegible] and the desolating progress either of Gengis or Napoleon? It is in vain to tell us that our knowledge of human nature is increased by the operation. *Useful* knowledge of that sort is acquired not by reading, but by experience; and with regard to political advantages, the less one knows of them the greater will be his delight in the principles of Lord Castlereagh and Sidmouth with their [illegible] suspension, holy league, and salvation of Europe. Yet, if not profit, there is some pleasure. In history, at all events, I believe we must not apply the *cui bono* too rigorously. It may be enough to sanction any pursuit that it gratifies an innocent, and still more an honorable, propensity of the human mind. When I look back upon this paragraph, I cannot but admit that reviewing is a very beneficial art. If a dull man take it into his head to write either for the press or the post-office without materials or a dead lift, it never fails to extricate him."

### 7.

*"May* 20, 1818.

" I believe it to be a truth (and though no creature believed it, it would continue to be a truth) that a man's dignity, in the great system of which he forms a part, is exactly proportioned to his moral and intellectual acquirements; and I find, moreover, that when I am assaulted by those feelings of discontent and ferocity which solitude at all times tends to pro-

duce, and by that host of miserable little passions
which are ever and anon attempting to disturb one's
repose, there is no method of defeating them so effectual as to take them in flank by a zealous course
of study. I believe all this, but my practice clashes
with my creed.

"* * * Sometimes, indeed, on a fine evening, and
when I have quenched my thirst with large potations
of Souchong, I say to myself, Away with despondency! Hast thou not a soul, and a kind of understanding in it? And what more has any analyst of
them all? But next morning, alas! when I consider
my understanding, how coarse yet feeble it is, and
how much of it must be devoted to supply the vulgar wants of life, or to master the paltry but never-
ending vexations with which all creatures are be-
leaguered, I ask how it is possible not to despond."

8.

*"July,* 1818.

"Be assured, I have not forgotten the many joyful days which long ago we spent together. Sweet
days of ignorance and airy hope! They had their
troubles too; but to bear them there was a light-
heartedness and buoyancy of soul which the sterner
qualities of manhood, and the hardier buffetings that
require them, have forever forbidden to return. I
forbear to say much of the pursuits which have en-

gaged me. They would little interest you, I fear. With most young men, I have had dreams of intellectual greatness, and of making me a name upon the earth. They were little else but dreams. To gain renown is what I do not hope, and hardly care for in the present state of my feelings. The improvement of one's mind, indeed, is the noblest object which can occupy any reasonable creature, but the attainment of it requires a concurrence of circumstances over which one has little control. I now perceive more clearly than ever that any man's opinions depend not on himself so much as on the age he lives in, or even the persons with whom he associates. If his mind at all surpass their habits, his aspirings are briefly quenched in the narcotic atmosphere that surrounds him. He forfeits sympathy, and provokes hatred, if he excel but a little the dull standard of his neighbors. Difficulties multiply as he proceeds, and none but chosen souls can rise to any height above the level of the swinish herd. Upon this principle, I could tell you why Socrates sacrificed at his death to Æsculapius; why Kepler wrote his 'Cosmographic Harmony;' and why Sir Thomas More believed the Pope to be infallible. Nevertheless, one should do what he can. I need not trouble you with the particulars of my situation. My prospects are not extremely brilliant at present. I have quitted all thoughts of the Church, for many

8

reasons, which it would be tedious, perhaps [illegible], to enumerate. I feel no love (I should wish to see the human creature that feels any love) for the paltry trade I follow; and there is before me a checkered and fluctuating scene, when I see nothing clearly, but that a little time will finish it. Yet wherefore should we murmur? A share of evil, greater or less (the difference of shares is not worth mentioning), is the unalterable doom of mortals, and the mind may be taught to abide in peace. Complaint is generally despicable, always worse than unavailing. It is an instructive thing, I think, to observe Lord Byron, surrounded with the voluptuousness of an Italian seraglio, chanting a mournful strain over the wretchedness of human life—and then to contemplate the poor but lofty-minded Epictetus, the slave of a cruel master too; and to hear him lifting up his voice to far-distant generations in the unforgotten words of his 'Encheiridion.' But a truce to moralizing; suffice it, with our Stoic, to suffer and abstain."

9.

"November, 1818.

"From the conversation which we had in the Inn of Basenthwaite, etc., I judge you are as unfit as myself for the study of theology, as they arrogantly name it. Whatever becomes of us, never let us cease to behave like honest men. * * *

"I have thought much and long of the irksome drudgery, the solitude, the gloom of my condition. I reasoned thus: These things may be endured, if not with a peaceful heart, at least with a serene countenance; but it is worth while to inquire whether the profit will repay the pain of enduring them—a scanty and precarious livelihood constitutes the profit; you know me and can form some judgment of the pain. But there is loss as well as pain. I speak not of the loss of health; but the destruction of benevolent feeling, that searing of the heart which misery, especially of a petty kind, sooner or later will never fail to effect—is a more frightful thing. The desire which, in common with all men, I feel for conversation and social intercourse is, I find, enveloped in a dense, repulsive atmosphere, not of vulgar *mauvaise-honte*, though such it is generally esteemed, but of deeper feelings, which I partly inherit from nature, and which are mostly due to the undefined station I have hitherto occupied in society. If I continue a schoolmaster, I fear there is little reason to doubt that these feelings will increase, and at last drive me entirely from the kindly sympathies of life, to brood in silence over the bitterness into which my friendly propensities must be changed. Where then would be my comfort? * * * I have thought of writing for booksellers. *Risum teneas;* for at times I am serious in this matter. In fine weather, it does strike me that there are in this head some ideas, a few *disjecta membra,* which might find admittance into some one of the many publications of the day. To live by authorship was never my intention. It is said not to be common at present, and happily so; for if we may credit biographies, the least miserable day of an author's life is generally the last.

> " '——sad cure, for who would lose,
> Though full of pain, this intellectual being,
> Those thoughts that wander through eternity,
> To perish rather, swallowed up and lost
> In the wide womb of uncreated night,
> Devoid of sense and motion ?'

\* \* \* You see, my boy, that my prospects are not the brightest in nature. Yet what shall we say? Contentment, that little‑practised virtue, has been inculcated by saint, by savage, and by sage—and by each person from a different principle. Do not fear that I shall read you a homily on that hackneyed theme. Simply I wish to tell you that in days of darkness—for there are days when my support (pride, or whatever it is) has enough to do—I find it useful to remember that Cleanthes whose [illegible] may last yet other two thousand years, never murmured when he labored by night, as a street-porter, that he might hear the lectures of Zeno by day; and that Epictetus, the ill‑used slave of a cruel tyrant's as wretched minion, wrote that 'Encheiridion' which may fortify the souls of the latest inhabitant of the earth. Besides, though neither of these men had adorned their species, it is morally certain that our earthly joys or griefs can last but for a few brief years; and though the latter were eternal, complaint and despondency could neither mitigate their intensity nor shorten their duration. Therefore, my duty and that of every young man on that point is clear as light itself."

10.

*"January 7, 1819.*

" * * * I wish from my soul some less laborious mode of friendly intercourse could be devised than letter-writing. Much may be done in the flight of ages; I despair of steam indeed, notwithstanding its felicitous application to many useful purposes, but who can limit the undiscovered agent with which knowledge is yet to enrich philanthropy? Charming prospect for the dull, above all, the solitary dull, of future times; small comfort for us, however, who, in no great fraction of one age, shall need to care nothing about the matter."

11.

" EDINBURGH, *February,* 1819.

" * * * I shall be much gratified to get intelligence of your fortunes. I might send you some details about my own, but they have nowise altered since I wrote last, and have therefore a most indefinite and wavering aspect. Your road through life seems to be separating from mine—perhaps never more to meet. During the five years that have elapsed since we lived together, each must have acquired principles and predilections in which the other cannot be expected to participate. Yet I trust, for the sake of both, that neither of us will cease to remember with a meek and kindly feeling that pleasant period which we spent together. Betide us what will, whenever we meet again may each see in the friend of his youth a man unsullied by anything that is paltry or degrading.

"Although well aware of the propensity which exists in men to speak more about themselves than others care for hearing, yet as you have hitherto been the participator of all my schemes, I venture to solicit your forbearance and advice at a time when I need them as much, perhaps, as I have ever done.

" * * * The source of that considerable quantity of comfort which I enjoy in these circumstances is twofold. First, there is the hope of better days, which I am not yet old or worn out enough to have quite laid aside.

" This cheerful feeling is combined with a portion of the universal quality which we ourselves name firmness, others obstinacy; the quality which I suppose to be the fulcrum of all Stoical philosophy, and which, when the charmer Hope has utterly forsaken us, may afford a grim support in the extreme of wretchedness. But there are other emotions which at times arise. When in my solitary walks round the Meadows or Carlton Hill, my mind escapes from the smoke and tarnish of those unfortunate persons with whom it is too much my fortune to associate; emotions which, if less fleeting, might constitute the principle of action, at once rational and powerful. It is difficult to speak upon these subjects without being ridiculous, if not hypocritical. Besides, the principles to which I allude, being little else than a more intense perception of certain truths universally acknowledged; to translate them into language would disgrace them to the rank of truisms. Therefore unwillingly I leave you to conjecture. It is probable, however, that your good-natured imagination might lead you to overrate my resources if I neglected to inform you that, upon the whole, my mind is far from philosophical composure. The vicissitudes of our opinions do not happen with the celerity or distinctness of an astronomical phenomenon; but it is evident that my mind at the present is undergoing sundry alterations. When I review my past conduct, it seems to have been guided by narrow or defective views, and (worst of all) by lurking, deeply lurking affectation. I could have defended these views by the most paramount logic; but what logic

can withstand experience? This is not the first, and
if I live long it will not be the last, of my revolutions.
Thus, *velut unda supervenit undam*, error succeeds to
error; and thus while I seek a rule of life, life itself
is fast flying away. At the last, perhaps, my creed
may be found too nearly to resemble the memorable
Tristrapædia of Walter Shandy, of which the minute
and indubitable directions for Tristram's baby-clothes
were finished when Tristram was in breeches. But
I forget the aphorism with which I began my letter.
Here, at least, let me conclude this long-winded account of my own affairs, and request from you as
particular a one of your own. We cannot help one
another, my friend; but mutual advice and encouragement may easily be given and thankfully received. Will you go to Liverpool, or Bristol, or
anywhither, and institute a classico - mathematical
academy? Or what say you to that asylum, or
rather hiding-place, of poverty and discontent, America? To be fabricating Lock No. 8 among the passes
of the Alleghany!"

[In the letter from which the above extract is
taken, Carlyle mentions that he is attempting to
learn German.]

12.

"EDINBURGH, 15 CARNEGIE STREET, *April*, 1819.

" The despicable wretchedness of teaching can be
known only to those who have tried it and to Him

who made the heart and knows it all. One meets with few spectacles more afflicting than that of a young man with a free spirit, with impetuous though honorable feelings, condemned to waste the flower of his life in such a calling; to fade in it by slow and sure corrosion of discontent; and, at last, obscurely and unprofitably to leave, with an indignant joy, the miseries of a world which his talents might have illustrated and his virtues adorned. Such things have been and will be. But surely in that better life which good men dream of, the spirit of a Kepler or a Milton will find a more propitious destiny.

"* * * I long to hear that you have comfortably adjusted your establishment in the Island of Man. In the event of your going thither, you have only to exert your abilities with the zeal and prudence of which you are capable; and I am convinced your hope of respectability and contentment will not be disappointed. Probably you are disposed to agree with the Pariah of Saint-Pierre, in thinking that "there is no real happiness without a good wife;" and it may be you are right. Let me advise you, however (you need not frown; I am not going to jest, but to give most serious and weighty counsel), to examine and re-examine the circumstances before taking any step in consequence of this persuasion. A calendar month destroys the illusions of the imagination; and if judgment be not interested, the rest of one's life

8*

is the very gall of bitterness. A narrow income, too!
It would break your heart—at least, I hope it would
—to see the helplessness of an amiable woman (grant-
ing that your choice was fortunate) exposed to the
hard [illegible] from which you had undertaken, but
were unable, to defend her. Of a truth, such a thing
should give us pause. But I doubt not your good
sense will render this advice superfluous. Your
good - nature will pardon it, considering the motive
which has called it forth. * * * As to my own
projects, I am sorry, on several accounts, that I can
give no satisfactory reply to your friendly inquiries.
A good portion of my life is already mingled with the
past eternity; and for the future—it is a dim scene,
on which my eyes are fixed as calmly and intensely
as possible—to no purpose. The probability of my
doing any service, in my day and generation, is certainly not very strong. Friends are necessary, and
I have few friends, and most of those few have their
own concerns to mind. Health also is requisite, but
my late precious trade and indolent habits (it must
be owned) have left me little of that to boast of."


### 13.

*"May*, 1819.

"It [first volume of Rousseau's "Confessions"] is
perhaps the most remarkable tome I ever read. Except for its occasional obscenity, I might wish to see

the remainder of the book, to try, if possible, to connect the character of Jean Jacques with my previous ideas of human nature. To say he is mad were to cut the knot without loosing it. At any rate, what could have induced any mortal, mad or wise, to recollect and delineate such a tissue of vulgar debauchery, false-heartedness, and misery is quite beyond my comprehension. If we regret our exclusion from that Gallic constellation, which has set and found no successor to its brilliancy, the 'Memoirs' of Marmontel or Rousseau's 'Confessions' should teach a virtuous Briton to be content with the dull sobriety of his native country."

## 14.

"*December,* 1819.

"Yet, in general, I set a stubborn front to the storm, live in hope of better days. In wet weather, indeed, when the digestive apparatus refuses to perform its functions, my world is sometimes black enough. Melancholy remembrances,

> " 'Shades of departed joys around me rise,
> With many a face that smiles on me no more,
> With many a voice that thrills of transport gave,
> Now silent as the grass that tufts their grave;'

and dark anticipations of the coming time—such are the fruits of solitude and want of settled occupation. But this, also, is vanity."

15.

"*March*, 1820.

"The thought that one's best days are hurrying darkly and uselessly away is yet more [illegible]. It is vain to deny it, my friend. I am altogether an —— creature. Timid, yet not humble; weak, yet enthusiastic, nature and education have rendered me entirely unfit to force my way among the thick-skinned inhabitants of this planet. Law, I fear, must be renounced; it is a shapeless mass of absurdity and chicane; and the ten years which a barrister commonly spends in painful idleness before arriving at employment is more than my physical and moral frame could endure. Teaching school is but another word for sure and not very slow destruction; and as to compiling the wretched lives of Montesquieu, Montaigne, Montagu, etc., for Dr. Brewster, the remuneration will hardly sustain life. But I touch a string which generally yields a tedious sound to any but the operator. I know you are not indifferent to the matter, but I would not tire you with it. The fate of one man is a mighty small concern in the grand whole, in this best of all possible worlds. Let us quit the subject with just one observation more, which I throw out for your benefit, should you ever come to need such an advice. It is to keep the profession you have adopted, if it be at all tolerable. A young

man who goes forth into the world to seek his fortune with those lofty ideas of honor and uprightness
which a studious, secluded life naturally begets will,
in ninety-nine cases out of the hundred, if friends
and other aids are wanting, fall into the sere, the
yellow leaf; and, if he quit not his integrity, end a
wretched, though happily a short, career in misery
and failure.

"I was glad to learn that you had finished the perusal of Homer. Certainly the blind bard is little
obliged by your opinion of him. I believe, however,
Candor is, and that is better. If from the admiration felt by Casaubon, Scaliger, and Co., and still more
by the crowds that blindly follow them, we could
subtract that portion which originates in the as hol-
low admiration of others for the same object; and
if, further, all affectation could be banished, I fear a
very inconsiderable item would remain. In fact,
Mæonides has had his day—at least the better part
of it; the noon was five-and-twenty centuries ago;
the twilight (for he set in 1453) may last for five-and-
twenty other centuries; but it, too, must terminate.
Nothing that we know of can last forever. The
very mountains are silently wasting away; and long
before eternity is done Mont Blanc might cease to
be the pinnacle of Europe, and Chimborazo lie under
the Pacific. Philosophy and literature have a far
shorter date. Error in the first succeeds to error, as

wave to wave.   Plato obscured the fame of Pythag-
oras; Cudworth and Kant, of Plato; the Stagyrite
and his idle spawn have been swept away by Lord
Bacon, himself to be swept away in his turn.   Even
in the narrow dominions of truth the continuance
of renown is not more durable; each succeeding observer from a higher vantage-ground compresses the
labors of his forerunner; and as the 'Principia' of
Newton is already swallowed up in the 'Mécanique
Céleste' of Laplace, so likewise will it fare with the
present Lord of the Ascendant.   Poetry, they tell
us, escapes the general doom; but, even without the
aid of revolutions or deluges, it cannot always escape.
The ideas about which it is conversant must differ
in every different age and country.   The poetry of
a Choctaw, I imagine, would turn chiefly on the pains
of hunger, and the pleasure of catching bears or
scalping Chickasaws.   In like manner, though some
of the affections which Homer delineates are coexist-
ent with the race, yet in the progress of refinement
(or change) his mode of delineating them will appear
trivial or disgusting, and the very twilight of his
fame will have an end.   Thus all things are dying,
my friend—only ourselves die faster!   Man! if I
had but £200 a year, a beautiful little house in some
laughing valley, three or four pure-spirited mortals
who would love me and be loved again, together with
a handsome library and—a great genius, I would in-

vestigate the hallucinations that connect themselves with such ideas. At present I must revisit this nether sphere."

16.

"MAINHILL, NEAR ECCLEFECHAN, *August* 4, 1820.

" * * * How could it have got into your head that you stood low in my estimation? The words that conveyed such an impression must indeed have been ill-chosen whenever they were used. Graglia's Dictionary and the rest came safely as well as timeously to hand; and though the articles had been entirely destroyed, do you think I would have quarrelled with you about so trifling an affair? It has been my chance to meet with *some* whose sympathy has brightened, at times, the gloomy labyrinth of life; but not to meet so many that I could sacrifice them upon grounds like this. I pray you put away such thoughts utterly. Our paths may lead us far asunder, but the place will be distant, the period remote, when I forget the calmness and happiness of bygone days, or the amiable qualities that contributed to make them calm and happy. I hope we shall meet together often, after all, when the sun is shining more brightly over us both; and I feel a sort of confidence that neither of us will allow his spirit to be sullied or debased, though disastrous twilight should still overcast both the present and the future.

" * * * My health has been indifferent for the

last three years—seldom *very* bad; I think it is im-
proving. My spirits, of course, have been various;
my prospects are a shadowy void. Yet why should
a living man complain? The struggle is brief; there
are short yet most sweet pauses in it; something of
pride, too, at times, will gild its humble endurance;
and there is all eternity to rest in.

"I could tell you much about the new Heaven and
new Earth which a slight study of German literature
has revealed to me; but room fails me, and time—
while 'twilight gray' and certain phenomena within
give warning that I should mount the sheltie and
take my evening ride."

### 17.

"*March*, 1821.

"* * * But toleration, man! Toleration is all I
ask, and all I am ready to give. Do you take your
Lipsius, your Crombie, your Schweighäuser, and let
me be doing with Lake Poets, Mystics, or any trash
I can fall in with. Why should we not cast an eye
of cheering, give a voice of welcome to each other as
our paths become mutually visible, though they are
no longer one? * * * The most enviable thing, I
often think, in all the world must be the soundest
of the Seven Sleepers; for he reposes deeply in his
corner, and to him the tragi-comedy of life is as
painless as it is paltry.

"* * * I have tried about twenty plans this winter in the way of authorship; they have all failed. I have about twenty more to try; and if it does but please the Director of all things to continue the moderate share of health now restored to me, I will make the doors of human society fly open before me yet, notwithstanding. My *petards* will not burst, or make only *noise* when they do. I must mix them better, plant them more judiciously; they shall burst and do execution, too.

"* * * I would not wish any one to launch, as I was forced to do, upon the roaring deep, so long as he can stay ashore. For me, the surges and the storm are round my skiff; yet I must on—on lest biscuit fail me, ere I reach the trade-wind and sail with others."

### 18.

*"April,* 1821.

"* * * I am moving on, weary and heavy-laden, with very fickle health, and many discomforts—still looking forward to the future (brave future!) for all the accommodation and enjoyment that render life an object of desire. *Then* shall I no longer play a candle-snuffer's part in the great drama; or if I do, my salary will be raised; *then shall*—which you see is just use and wont."

19.

"*October*, 1821.

"* * * My own experience of these things is trifling and unfavorable; yet I do not reckon the problem of succeeding in a school, and learning to remedy and endure all its grievances, one of extreme difficulty. First, as in every undertaking, it is necessary, of course, that you wish to succeed; that you determine firmly to let nothing break your equanimity, that you 'lay aside every weight'—your philosophical projects, your shyness of manner (if you are cursed with that quality), your jealous sense of independence—everything, in short, that circumstances may point out as detrimental to your interest with the people; and then, being thus balanced and set in motion, your sole after-duty is to 'run with patience;' you will reach the goal undoubtedly. Public favor in some sense is requisite for all men, but a teacher ought constantly to bear in mind that it is life and breath to *him*. Hence, in comparison with it nothing should be dear to him; he must be meek and kindly, and soft of speech to every one, how absurd or offensive soever. To the same object he must also frequently sacrifice the real progress of his pupils, if it cannot be gained without affecting their peace of mind. The advantages of great learning are so vague and distant, the miseries of constant whining are so immediate and manifest, that not one parent in a thousand can take the former in exchange for the latter, with patience—not to speak of thankfulness. For the same reason, he must (if the fashion of the place require it) go about and visit his employers; he must cook them and court them by every innocent mode which the ever-varying posture of circumstances will suggest to a mind on the outlook for them. This seems poor philosophy, but it is true. The most diligent fidelity in discharging your duties will not serve you—by itself. Never forget this—it is mathematically certain. If men were angels, or even purely intellectual beings, having judgment, but no vanity or other passion, it might be different; but as it is, the case becomes much more complicated. Few, very few, had not rather be cheated than despised; and even in the common walks of life, probity is often left to rot, without so much as being praised. It has the *alget* without the *laudatur*, which is a most sorry business, doubtless. I have written down all this, my dear ——, not because I thought you wanted it; on the contrary, I imagine your talents and manners and temper promise you a distinguished success; but because I thought the fruit of my painful experience might be worth something to you, and that something, however small, I was anxious to offer you. Take it, and call it the *widow's mite*, if you like. It is from your friend, T. CARLYLE."

20.

" * * * It is a great truth which Gibbon sets forth somewhere, that letters are like alms, in one respect—symbols of friendship, as alms are of charity, though it is well known that the thing signified may exist in great activity without the symbol, in both cases. At all events, I hope you need no persuasion that I feel always great pleasure in writing to you; not only as to a man whose talents and principle I respect, but also as to one with whom some of the most picturesque years of my life are inseparably connected in memory; whose name recalls to me a thousand images of the past, a thousand passages and half-forgotten moods of mind, which were not without a degree of pleasure while present, and which distance is every day rendering dearer, and covering with a softer and purer color. How many sheets have I scrawled to you, how many consultations and merrymakings and loungings have we had together! How many sage purposes and speculations have we formed by each other's counsel—how contentedly, though neither of us knew the right hand from the left! I declare I shall always think of those days with a certain melancholy pleasure, and keep anticipating the nights when we (old gray-heads, covered with honor as with years) shall yet sit by each other's hearth, and recount these achievements, and forget, in recollecting them, all the weakness and the weariness and cares and coldnesses of age. 'Châteaux en Espagne,' you say. No matter, they look very hospitable, and one loves to gaze upon them.

"* * * One thing I am sure of, and congratulate you upon: it is the advantage you possess over me in having a fixed object in life; a kind of chart of the course you are to follow, and the opportunity not only of enjoying all the pleasures which this affords in the meantime, but likewise of increasing your experience, and thus at once, by the power of habit and of new skill in discharging your duties, increasing and accumulating more and more your means of happiness and usefulness. There is an immense blessing in your lot. I advise you (for two good reasons) to beware of letting it go. None but a wandering, restless pilgrim, who has travelled long and advanced little, anxious to proceed on his destined journey, but perpetually missing or changing his path, can tell you how fine a thing it is to have a beaten turnpike for your accommodation. Better to keep it, almost however miry and rugged, than to spring the hedge, and so lose yourself among footpaths."

21.

"I need not advise you to keep a strict watch over your health; you have already suffered too severely to need any such caution. The whole earth has no blessing within its circuit worthy to be named along with health. The loss of it I reckon the very dearest item in the lot of man. I often think I could snap my fingers in the face of everything, if it were not for this. Pandora's box was but a toy compared with biliousness, or any other fundamental bodily disorder. *Watch!* watch! and think *mens sana in corpore sano* is the whole concern.

"They [the probationers of the Scottish Kirk] are getting into kirks gradually, or lingering on the muddy shore of 'Private Teaching,' to see if any Charon will waft them across the Styx of Patronage into the Elysium of teinds and glebe. Success attend them all, poor fellows! They are cruising in one small sound, as it were, of the great ocean of life; their trade is harmless, their vessels leaky; it will be hard if they altogether fail. * * * I sit here and read all the morning, or write; regularly burning everything I write. It is a hard matter that one's thoughts should be so poor and scanty, and at the same time the power of uttering them so difficult to acquire.

"* * * Have you seen the *Liberal?* It is a most happy performance. Byron has a 'Vision of Judgment' there; and a 'Letter to the Editor of my Grandmother's Review,' of the wickedest and cleverest turn you could imagine. * * * This is a wild, fighting, loving, praying, blaspheming, weeping, laughing sort of world!"

### 22.

"KENNAIRD HOUSE, *June* 17, 1823.

"Your letters have a charm to me, independently of their intrinsic merit. They are letters of my first and oldest correspondent; they carry back the mind to old days—days perhaps in themselves not greatly better than those now passing over us, but invested by the kind treachery of imagination with hues which nothing present can equal. If I have any fault to find with you it is in the very excess of what renders any correspondence agreeable—the excess of your complaisance, the too liberal [word wanting] which you offer at the shrine of other people's vanity. I might object to this with the more asperity did I not consider that flattery is in truth the sovereign emollient, the true oil of life, by which the joints of the great social machine, often stiff and rusty enough, are kept from grating, and made to play sweetly to and fro; hence, that if you pour it on a thought too lavishly, it is an error on the safe side—an error which

proceeds from the native warmness of your heart,
and ought not to be quarrelled with too sharply; not,
at least, by one who profits, though unduly, by the
commission of it. So I will submit to be treated as
a kind of slender genius, since my friend will have
it so. Our intercourse will fare but little worse on
that account. We have now, as you say, known each
other long, and never, I trust, seen aught to make us
ashamed of that relation. I calculate that succeeding years will but more firmly establish our connection, strengthening with the force of habit, and the
memory of new kind offices, what has a right to subsist without those aids. Some time hence, when you
are seated in your peaceful manse—you at one side
of the parlor fire, Mrs. M. at the other, and two or
three little M.'s, fine chubby urchins, hopping about
the carpet—you will suddenly observe the door fly
open, and a tall, meagre, care-worn figure stalk forward, his grim countenance lightened by unusual
smiles, in the certainty of meeting with a cordial
welcome. This knight of the rueful visage will, in
fact, mingle with the group for a season, and be
merry as the merriest, though his looks are sinister.
I warn you to make provision for such emergencies.
In process of time, I, too, must have my own peculiar
hearth; wayward as my destiny has hitherto been,
perplexed and solitary as my path of life still is, I
never cease to reckon on yet paying scot and lot on

my own footing. Like the men of Glasgow, I shall
have 'a house within myself' (what tremendous *ab-
domina* we householders have!) with every suitable
appurtenance, before all is done; and when friends
are met, there is little chance that will be forgotten.
We shall talk over old times, compare old hopes with
new fortune, and secure comfort by Sir John Sin-
clair's celebrated recipe, *by being comfortable.* There
are certainly brave times: would they could only be
persuaded to come on a little faster.

"Dunkeld is about the prettiest village I ever beheld. I shall not soon forget the bright sunset, when
skirting the base of the " Birnam Wood " (there is no
wood now) and asking for Dunsinane's high hill,
which lies far to the eastward, and thinking of the
immortal link-boy who has consecrated those two
spots, which he never saw, with a glory that [will
last] forever. I first came in sight of the ancient
capital of Caledonia, standing in the lap of the
mountains, with its quick broad river running by—
its old gray cathedral, and its peak - roofed white
houses peering through many groves of stately trees,
all gilded from the glowing west—the whole so clear
and pure and gorgeous as if it had been a city of
fairy - land; not a vulgar *clachan,* where men sell
stots, and women buy eggs by the dozen. I walked
round and round it till late, the evening I left you.
* * * The virtue of punctuality [is not considered]
9

in treatises of Ethics, but it is of essential importance in the conduct of life; like common kitchen-
salt, scarce heeded by cooks and purveyors, though
without it their wares would soon run to rottenness
and ruin."

### 23.

" * * * I quitted the muddy beach of my native
Scotland, 'stern nurse for a dyspeptic child,' with no
other feelings towards it than I had long entertained.  Hard, rugged land!  I often think of its earnest
features amid the rich scenes of the south.  Distance
is producing something of its usual effect: much
that was unpleasant or repulsive is forgotten or softened down; and I think of the green landscape of
Perthshire or the bleak simplicity of Annandale,
which the sight of them was often far from giving.
London astonishes, disgusts, and charms me.  There
are two or three persons there whom I should regret
to know no more about.

" * * * ⸺ ⸺ is not a Scotchman. * * * Hard-
ship, I suspect, has withered out the sensibilities of
his nature, and turned him, finally, into a whisking,
antithetical little editor.  There is no significance in
his aspect.  His blue frock, and switch, and fashion-
able wig, and clear, cold eyes, and clipt accents, and
slender *persiflage* might befit a dandy. * * * Allan
Cunningham I love: he retains the honest tones of

his native Nithsdale true as ever. He has a heart; a mind simple as a child's, but with touches of genius singularly wild and original. —— —— is a kind little fellow, sings Italian airs, keeps daggers and other play-gear lying on his dressing-table, and is of the mob of gentlemen who write with ease. —— —— sprawls about as if his body consisted of four ill-conditioned flails. Coleridge is a steam - engine of a hundred horses' power, with the boiler burst. His talk is resplendent with imagery and the shows of thought; you listen as to an oracle, and find yourself no jot the wiser. He is without beginning or middle or end. * * * A round, fat, oily, yet impatient little man, his mind seems totally beyond his own control; he speaks incessantly, not thinking or [illegible] remembering, but combining all these processes into one, as a lazy housewife might mingle her soup and fish and beef and custard into one unspeakable mass, and present it true-heartedly to her astonished guest."

24.

"SCOTSBRIG, *June* 20, 1826.

"* * * Be in no haste for a church; and feel very happy that you can do very comfortably without one, till the time come—whenever that may be. I begin to see that one is fifty times better for being heartily drilled in the school of experience, though beaten daily for years with forty stripes save one.

I used to reckon myself very wretched, and now I
find that no jot of my castigation could have been
spared."

25.

" 21 COMLEY BANK ROW,
EDINBURGH, *December* 12, 1827.

" MY DEAR SIR,—My mother is arrived here on a
short visit to us, and feels extremely anxious, among
other purposes, to see her old friend, your aunt, Mrs.
Hope, whom she parted with in Ecclefechan, many
years ago, with very little expectation of ever meeting her again. I think you once told me the old
lady lived somewhere in the outskirts of this city;
if so, it will not be impossible to bring about this interview, in which I myself feel somewhat interested,
having still a vivid recollection of that disastrous gig
expedition which I executed under your auspices on
the Moffatt Road. Will you be so good as to send
us a note of Mrs. Hope's address, and let us try if we
can find her? The sooner the better, for my mother's time is limited.

" I dare say you come often to Edinburgh: how is
it that you never find your way to Comley Bank?
Come hither, and I will show you my little cottage,
and introduce you to my little wife, who will receive
you with all graciousness as her husband's friend.
Come down the very first time you visit Edinburgh.
There is a spare bed here, and many a reminiscence
of auld lang-syne.

"I am grown quite a stranger in Glasgow of late years, now that Grahame and Irving and all have left it: yet the memory of that hospitable, jolly, well-living city still dwells with me fresh as ever, and hopes that a time is coming when I may behold it again. Meanwhile my true prayer is, in the words of your civic emblazonry, Let Glasgow flourish! and you and all the honest hearts that have your being in it.

"My mother brings no tidings from Grahame, except that he is still at Burnswark, irrigating meadows, salting bog hay, and striving by agricultural philosophy to make 'the desert blossom as the rose.' I heard that he had hopes of returning to your city and resuming traffic. I pray that it may be so, for it is a thousand pities so good and gifted a man were not working in his proper sphere, where alone he can be happy and wholesomely active.

"I have heard several times from the Caledonian orator of late. He does *not* seem in the least millenniary in his letters: but the same old friendly man we have long known him to be. And yet his printed works are enough to strike one blank with amazement: for if the millennium is to come upon us in twenty years and odd months, ought we not to be turning a new leaf? ought not you to shut up your ledger and I my note-book, and both of us to sit on the lookout, like Preventive-service men, spying and

scenting, with eye and nostril, whether there be
aught of it in the wind? Alas! alas! the madness
of man findeth no termination, but only new shapes,
the old spirit being still the same. To the last there
is and will be a bee in his bonnet, which only in
every new generation buzzes with a new note.

"I am scribbling here with considerable diligence,
and not without satisfaction, though still in very poor
health. In the course of years I hope to grow better; but now, such is the extent of my philosophy,
I think I can partly do, whether I get better or not.
My brother John, the doctor, is away in Germany,
dissecting *subjects*, I suppose, at this very date, in
Munich, the capital of Bavaria. He writes to us full
of wonder at the marvels of that strange land. Mrs.
C. and I have some thoughts of going thither and
winter ourselves. But why should I darken counsel
by words without wisdom? Send us that address of
Mrs. Hope as soon as possible; come over to Comley
Bank the first day or night you are in town; and
believe me ever, my dear sir,

"Affectionately yours,

"Thomas Carlyle."

26.

"Craigenputtoch, *May* 31, 1828.

"* * * O Murray! how we poor sons of Adam
are shovelled to and fro! Do you remember when
we walked together, you escorting me, to the fifth

mile-stone on the Dumfries road? Two young pilgrims; yet even then the future looking stern and fateful in our eyes! How many a weary foot have we had to travel since that hour! and here we are still travelling, and must travel till the sun set and we get to our inn! Well, let us travel cheerily; for, after all, it is a brave journey: the great universe is around us; time and space are ours; and in that city whither we are bound it is said 'there are many mansions.' "

## 27.

TO —— FERGUSON.

"ANNAN, *October* 22, 1820.

"MY DEAR FERGUSON,—I delayed writing to you chiefly for the old reason—want of anything to say; and I have begun to write not because that want is at all sufficiently supplied, but because I would not vex your mind by unfounded suspicions that absence and oblivion are interchangeable terms in my vocabulary, or that the light of two months' experience has shown me any flaws in your character to the prejudice of our wavering though agreeable (*sic*) correspondence. I prize the frankness of your procedure in writing a second time; there is so much of the counting-house in formal regularity, one likes to see a friend's letter sometimes want the 'I duly received your valuable favor, dated, and so forth.' It is not my inclination to put your generosity often to such trials; but I promise you the present exercise of it shall not be thrown away.

" The first letter, written late, appears also to have lingered long on the road. It reached me while in the heat of managing a small concern, which not long after called me into Yorkshire; and I wilfully delayed sending an answer, till, the affair being finally adjusted, I might have it in my power to communicate what seemed then likely to produce a considerable change in my stile (*sic*) of life. The matter I allude to was a proposal to become 'a travelling tutor,' as they call it, to a young person in the North Riding, for whom that exercise was recommended, on account of bodily and mental weakness. They offered me £150 per annum, and withal invited me to come and examine things on the spot, before engaging. I went, accordingly, and happy was it I went. From description, I was ready to accept the place; from inspection, all Earndale would not have hired me to accept it. This boy was a dotard, a semivegetable; the elder brother, head of the family, a two-legged animal without feathers, intellect, or virtue; and all the connections seemed to have the power of eating pudding, but no higher power. So I left the barbarous people—kindly, however, because they used me kindly, and crossed the Sark, with a higher respect for our own bleak fatherland than ever I had felt before. York is but a heap of bricks;

Jonathan Dryasdust (see 'Ivanhoe') is justly named. It was edifying to hear the principal of their Unitarian College lament the prevalence of mysticism in religion; and as to their newspaper editor, though made of lead, he is lighter than McCullogh's little finger. York is the Bœotia of Britain; its inhabitants enjoy all sensual pleasures in perfection; they have not even the idea of any other. Upon the whole, however, I derived great amusement from my journey. I viewed a most rich and picturesque country. I conversed with all kinds of men, from graziers up to knights of the shire; argued with them all, and broke specimens from the souls (if any), which I retain within the museum of my cranium for your inspection at a future day.

" It is scarce a week since I returned from this expedition; and now my plans must all be altered. If I come to Edinburgh, which seems likely, few manuscripts will accompany or follow me; no settled purpose will direct my conduct, and the next scene of this fever dream is likely to be as painful as the last. Expect no account of my prospects there, for I have no prospects that are worth the name. I am like a being thrown from another planet on this dark terrestrial ball, an alien, a pilgrim among its possessors; I have no share in their pursuits; and life is to me like a pathless, a waste, and howling wilderness—surface barrenness, its verge enveloped under 'dark-

9*

brown shade.' Yet hope will sometimes visit me, and, at the worst, complaint is weak, and idle if it were not. After all, one has a desperate struggle— and for what? For the bubble reputation, that we may fly alive through the mouths of men, and be thought happy, or learned, or great, by creatures as feeble and fleeting as ourselves. Sure it is a sorry recompense for so much [illegible] bustle and vexation. Do not leave your situation, if you can possibly avoid it. Experience shows it to be a fearful thing to be swept on by the roaring surge of life, and then to float alone—undirected on its restless, monstrous bosom. Keep ashore while yet you may; or, if you must to sea, sail under convoy; trust not the waves without a guide. You and I are but pinnaces or cockboats yet; hold fast by the Manilla ship; *do not let go* the painter, however rough and grating. I am sorry you are tired of anatomy, and such things. I am tired too, but that does not mend the matter. Yet trust the best; *nec deus intersit* is indeed true, naturally as well as poetically. Yet in spite of this, all things will and shall be well, if we believe aright. I designed to tell you a long tale about my most neglected studies, but I have no room. I have lived riotously with Schiller, Goethe, and the rest. They are the greatest men at present with me,

"I am yours affectionately,

"T. CARLYLE."

## 28.

"Craigenputtoch, Dumfries, *November* 20, 1832.

"My dear Sir,—I sent you a little note, by some conveyance I had, several months ago; whether it ever came to hand is unknown here. We learned soon afterwards, from a notice in the *New Monthly Magazine*, that you were again suffering in health.

"If that note reached you, let this be the second; if it did not, let this be the first little messenger arriving from the mountains to inquire for you, to bring assurance that you are lovingly remembered here, that nothing befalling you can be indifferent to us.

"Being somewhat uncertain about the number of your house, I send this under cover to a friend who will punctually see that it reaches its address. If he deliver it in person, as is not impossible, you will find him worth welcoming. He is John Mill, eldest son of India Mill; and, I may say, one of the best, clearest-headed, and clearest-hearted young men now living in London.

"We sometimes fancy we observe you in Tait's and other periodicals. Have the charity sometime soon to send us a token of your being and well-being. We often speak of you here, and are very obstinate in remembering.

"I still wish much you would write Hazlitt's Life. Somewhat of history lay in that too luckless man; and you, of all I can think of, have the organ for discerning it and delineating it.

"As for myself, I am doing little. The literary element is one of the most confused to live in, at all times; the bibliopolic condition of this time renders it perfect chaos. One must write 'articles'—write and curse (as Ancient Pistol ate his leek); what can one do?

"My wife is not with me to-day, otherwise she would surely beg to be remembered. You will offer my best wishes to Mrs. Hunt, to Miss, and the little gray-eyed philosopher who listened to us.

"I asked you to come hither and see us, whenever you wanted to rusticate a month. Is that forever impossible?

"I remain, always, my dear sir, yours truly and kindly, T. CARLYLE."

29.

"CRAIGENPUTTOCH, *April* 18, 1834.

"MY DEAR SIR,—Your letters are rare, too rare, in their outward quality of sequence through the post; but happily still rarer in their inward quality; the hope and kind trustful sympathy of new eighteen dwelling unworn under hair which, you tell me, is getting tinged with gray. It is actually true we are coming to London! So far has Destiny and a little resolution brought it. The kind Mrs. Austin, after search enough, has now (we imagine) found us a house which I hope and believe is not very far from yours. It shall be farther than my widest calculation if I fail to meet your challenge, and walk and talk with you to all lengths. I know not well how Chelsea lies from the Parish Church of Kensington, but it is within sight of the latter we are to be; and some 'trysting-tree' (do you know so much Scotch?) is already getting into leaf, as yet unconscious of its future honor between these two suburbs of Babylon. Some days, too, we will walk the whole day long, in wide excursion; you lecturing me on the phenomena of the region, which to you are native. My best amusement is walking; I like, as well as Hadrian himself, to mete out my world with steps of my own, and to take possession of it. But if to this you add Speech! Is not Speech defined to be cheerfuller than light, and the eldest daughter of Heaven? I mean articulate discourse of reason, that comes from the internal heavenly part of us; not the confused gabble, which (in so many millions) comes from no deeper than the palate of the mouth, which it is the saddest of all things to listen to—a thing that fills one alternately with sorrow and indignation, and at last almost with a kind of horror and terror.

As if the world were a huge Bedlam, and the sacred speech of men had become an inarticulate jargon of hungry, cawing rooks!

" We laid down your description of your house as the model our kind friend was to aim at. How far we have prospered will be seen. In rent we are nearly on a par. We also anticipate quiet, and some visitations of the heavenly air; but, for the rest, ours will be no 'high-wainscoted' dwelling, like Homer's and yours—no, some new-fangled brickwork which will tremble at every step, in which no four-footed thing can stand, but only three-footed, such as 'Holland Street, Kensington,' in this year of grace, can be expected to yield. However, there is a patch of garden, or, indeed, two patches. I shall have some little crib for my books and writing-table, and so do the best that may be. Innumerable vague forebodings hang over me as I write; meanwhile there is one grand assurance—the feeling that it was a duty, almost a necessity. My dame, too, is of resolution for the enterprise, and whatsoever may follow it; so, forward in God's name!

" I have seen nothing of you for a long time, except what of the ' Delicacies of Pig-driving' my *Examiner* once gave me. A most tickling thing, not a word of which can I remember; only the whole *fact* of it, pictured in such subquizzical, sweet-acid geniality of mockery, stands here, and, among smaller and greater things, will stand. If the two volumes are of that quality, they will be worth a welcome. I cannot expect them now till the beginning of May; or perhaps I may even still find them with Fraser at Whitsuntide. Here among the moors they were best of all.

" The starting of your *Journal* was a glad event for me; it seems one of the hopefullest projects in these days: and surely it must be a strange public, one would think, in which —— —— prospers and Leigh Hunt fails. You must bear up steadily *at first;* it is there, in this as in all things, that the grand difficulties lie.

" Thornton need be under no uneasiness about Henry Inglis, from whom we heard not long ago, with some remark, too, of a very friendly character, about the traveller in question, and not the faintest hint about pounds or shillings.

" I am writing *nothing;* reading, above all things, my old Homer and Prolegomena enough; the old song itself with a most singular delight. Fancy me as reading till you see me; then must *another* scene open. Your newspapers will interest me; as for the unhappy ' Sartor,' none can detest him more than my present self. There are some ten pages rightly *fused* and harmonious; the rest is only *welded,* or even agglomerated, and may be thrown to the swine. All salutations from us both!

" *Valete et nos amate!*      T. CARLYLE."

30.*

"DEAR HUNT,—I have just finished your 'Autobiography,' which has been most pleasantly occupying all my leisure these three days; and you must permit me to write you a word upon it, out of the fulness of the heart, while the impulse is still fresh, to thank you. This good book, in every sense one of the best I have read this long while, has awakened many old thoughts which never were extinct, or even properly asleep, but which (like so much else) have had to fall silent amid the tempests of an evil time— Heaven mend it! A word from me once more, I know, will not be unwelcome while the world is talking of you.

"Well, I call this an excellent good book, by far the best of the autobiographic kind I remember to have read in the English language; and, indeed, except it be Boswell's of Johnson, I do not know where we have such a picture drawn of human life as in these three volumes.

"A pious, ingenious, altogether human and worthy book, imaging, with graceful honesty and free felic-

---

* This letter, though most of it appeared in an edition of Leigh Hunt's "Autobiography," is here for the first time printed *verbatim*, and therefore included among others which appear here for the first time.

ity, many interesting objects and persons on your life-path, and imaging throughout, what is best of all, a gifted, gentle, patient, and valiant human soul, as it buffets its way through the billows of the time, and will not drown, though often in danger; cannot be drowned, but conquers, and leaves a track of radiance behind it: that, I think, comes out more clearly to me than in any other of your books; and that, I can venture to assure you, is the best of all results to realize in a book or written record. In fact, this book has been like an exercise of devotion to me; I have not assisted at any sermon, liturgy or litany, this long while, that has had so religious an effect on me. Thanks in the name of all men! And believe, along with me, that this book will be welcome to other generations as well as ours. And long may you live to write more books for us; and may the evening sun be softer on you (and on me) than the noon sometimes was!

"Adieu, dear Hunt (you must let me use this familiarity, for I am now an old fellow too, as well as you). I have often thought of coming up to see you once more; and perhaps I shall, one of these days (though horribly sick and lonely, and beset with spectral lions, go whitherward one may); but, whether I do or not, believe forever in my regard. And so God bless you! prays heartily T. CARLYLE."

31.

"CHELSEA, *June* 21.

"DEAR HUNT,—Many kind thanks! I saw the book, and sent thanks for it by Vincent; but I did not know, till this minute, what other pleasant things lay in the letter itself, which the dusk and the hurry would not suffer me to read at the moment. By all means, yes, yes! My wife is overjoyed at the prospect of seeing you again in the good old style. Courage, and do not disappoint us. We are here, quite disengaged, and shall be right glad to see you.

"I hope Vincent explained what a miscellaneous uproar had accidentally got about me to-night, and how for want of light, as well as of time, I missed the kernel of the letter altogether. Tuesday, remember! We dine about five, and tea comes naturally about seven—sooner if you will come sooner.

"One of my people to-night, an accomplished kind of American, has begged a card of introduction to you. He is a son of a certain noted Judge Story; is himself, I believe, a kind of sculptor and artist, as well as lawyer. Pray receive him if he call; you will find him a friendly and entertainable and entertaining man.

"And so, till Tuesday evening,

"Yours with all regard,

"T. CARLYLE."

## 32.

### TO WILLIAM BRIDGES.

"CHELSEA, *November* 19, 1846.

"MY DEAR SIR,—I have read your letter, 'History in a Nutshell,' with much pleasure. It is surely an eloquent, pious, melodious conception of that immeasurable matter; and, if you chose to elaborate it further, might lead you into all manner of interesting analogies and contrasts. I like well, in particular, that co-ordinating of sacred events with events called 'Profane.' We ought to know always that if any one of them be sacred, they are all sacred. That is the right use to make of the, at present, very burdensome 'Hebrew element' in our affairs. In this way we shall conquer it, not let it conquer us— which latter is a very bad result, worse even than running from it; as the world in these centuries, as a *bad-best*, is very much inclined to do. I should be glad to know more minutely what you are about of late; and to see you here some evening when you feel inclined to walk so far.

"Yours very truly,

"T. CARLYLE."

## 33.

### TO A LITERARY FRIEND.

"THE GRANGE, ALRESFORD, HANTS, *September* 26, 1848.

"DEAR ——,—I know not what little tiff this is
that has arisen between —— and you, but I wish
much it would handsomely blow over, and leave all
of you in the simple state of as you were. Reflect-
ing on the enclosed little note that reached me this
morning, I decide that one of the usefullest things I
could, in the first place, attempt in regard to it would
be to try if hereby the matter could not be quashed,
and people who are certainly good friends, and who
are probably of real service to one another, be prevented from flying asunder on slight cause.

"This controversy I know well enough to be perpetual and universal between Editor and Contributor: no law can settle it; the best wisdom can do
no better than suppress it from time to time. On
——'s side I will counsel patience, everywhere needful in human affairs; on your side, I would say that
though an editor can never wholly abandon his right
to superintend, which will mean an occasional right
to alter, or at least to remonstrate and propose alterations, yet it is in general wise, when, as in this case,
you have got a really conscientious, accurate, and
painstaking contributor, to be sparing in the exercise
of the right, and to put up with various unessential

things rather than *forcibly* break in to amend them. You have perhaps but a faint idea how much it distresses and disheartens such a man as I describe; nay, lames him in the practice of his art, and tends to put his conscience especially into painful abeyance. 'What is the use of me?' his literary conscience says; 'better for us all that I went to sleep.' When a man *has* a literary conscience—which I believe is a very rare case—this result is a most sad one to bring about; hurtful not to himself only, as you may well perceive. In fact, I think a serious sincere man *cannot* very well write if he have the perpetual fear of correction before his eyes; and if I were the master of such a one, I should certainly endeavor to leave him (within very wide limits) his own director, and to let him feel that he was so, and responsible accordingly.

"Forgive me if I interfere unduly with your affairs. If the case be that you perceive, after the trial, that —— is no longer worth his wages to the ——, then all is said, and I have not a word to object. But if it be not so, and this is but a transitory embarrassment of detail, then it will be a service to both parties if I can get it ended within the safe limits. Of the fact, how it may stand, I know nothing at all, and you alone can know.

"All help that I can give —— in other courses of enterprise I have, of course, to promise him; but I will advise him first of all that a reconciliation with you, if any ground he feels feasible were offered, would seem to me by far the desirablest course. With kind regards to ——, to whom, indeed, as much as to you, these remarks address themselves, in great haste, yours, always truly,          T. CARLYLE."

" We have been here with country friends near a month, and are not to be in Chelsea, I imagine, for some ten days.          T. C."

34.

TO ALEXANDER IRELAND.

"CHELSEA, *October* 15, 1847.

" MY DEAR SIR,—By a letter I had very lately from Emerson — which had lain, lost and never missed, for above a month in the treacherous post-office of Buxton, where it was called for and denied—I learn that Emerson intended to sail for this country 'about the first of October,' and infer therefore that probably even now he is near Liverpool or some other of our ports. Treadmill, or other as emphatic admonition, to that scandalous postmaster of Buxton! He has put me in extreme risk of doing one of the most unfriendly and every way unpardonable-looking things a man could do.

"Not knowing in the least to what port Emerson is tending, where he is expected, or what his first engagements are, I find no way of making my word audible to him in time, except that of intrusting it, with solemn charges, to you, as here. Pray do me the favor to contrive in some sure way that Emerson may get hold of that note the instant he lands in England. I shall be permanently grieved otherwise; shall have failed in a clear duty (were it nothing more) which will never probably in my life offer itself again. Do not neglect, I beg very much of you; and, on the whole, if you can get Emerson put safe into the express train, and shot up hither, as the first road he goes! That is the result we aim at. But the note itself, at all events, I pray you get that delivered duly, and so do me a very great favor for which I depend on you.

"It is yet only two days since I got home, through Keswick and the Lake country; nor has my head yet fairly settled from the whirl of so many objects, and such rapid whirls of locomotion, outward and inward, as the late weeks have exposed me to. Today, therefore, I restrict myself to the indispensable, and will add nothing more.

"Kind regards to Ballantyne and Espinasse. Hope your School Society prospers. Glad shall I be to learn that your scheme, or any rational or even semi-rational scheme, for that most urgently needful object, promises to take effect among those dusty populations! Of your Program, as probably I mentioned, there remains with me no copy now.

"Yours very truly,    T. CARLYLE."

35.

"DEAR IRELAND,—I am glad to hear from you again, and much obliged for those two portraits of Emerson. The painted one I cannot endure, but the actual shadow of *the sun* (who aims at nothing but the truth) is beautiful, and really interesting to me. Wonderfully little oldened; has got a black wig, I see; nothing else changed!

" Two or three weeks ago there was forwarded to me a clipping from a Manchester newspaper (the *Examiner*, I think)—some letter from somebody about a wonderful self-condemnatory MS. by Frederick the Great, gathered at Berlin by some Duke of Rovigo, for the endless gratitude of the curious. I had not heard of the monstrous platitude at all till then, but guessed then what it would be—an old acquaintance of mine, truly a thrice-brutal stupidity, which has had red-hot pokers indignantly run through it about ten times, but always revives and steps forth afresh with new tap of the parish drum—there being no ' parish' in the universe richer in prurient darkness and flunkey malevolence than ours is! I set Neuberg upon it, in the *Athenæum*, but know not what he made of it. No editor, in my time, has crowned himself with such a pair of ears as he of the Williams and Norgate periodical. It is a clear fact, though not clear in England, that here is the *most* brutal of moon-calves lately heard of in any country; that to have one moment's belief, or doubt, on such a subject is to make affidavit that your knowledge of Frederick and his affairs is zero and *less*. Would to Heaven I were 'done with them!' I never in my life was held in such hurry—to last six months yet.                    Yours ever,        T. CARLYLE."

## 36.*

### TO A YOUNG LADY FRIEND.

"5 GREAT CHEYNE ROW, CHELSEA, 21*st*, 1866.

"DEAR YOUNG LADY,—Your appeal to me is very touching, and I am heartily sorry for you, if I could but help at all. In very great want of time, among other higher requisites, I write a few words, which, I hope, may at least do no harm, if they can do little good. Herein, as in many other cases, the 'patient must minister unto himself;' no best of doctors can do much. The grand remedy against such spiritual maladies and torments is to rise upon them vigorously from without, in the way of practical work

---

* This letter is not in Mr. Ireland's collection. It was written to a lady of my acquaintance when she was quite a young girl. She had passed into a somewhat morbid state of mind and feeling about herself, and wrote to the man who appeared to her almost a prophet. The letter reveals that tenderness of Carlyle towards the young which was really the unsatisfied part of his nature, as I believe was recognized by him towards the last.—M. D. C.

and performance. Our thoughts, good or bad, are not in our command, but every one of us has at all hours duties to *do*, and these he can do negligently, like a slave; or faithfully, like a true servant. '*Do* the duty that is nearest thee'—that first, and that well; all the rest will disclose themselves with increasing clearness, and make their successive demand. Were your duties never so small, I advise you, set yourself with double and treble energy and punctuality to do them, hour after hour, day after day, in spite of the devil's teeth! That is our one answer to all inward devils, as they used to be called. 'This I *can* do, O Devil, and I do it, thou seest, in the name of God.' It is astonishing and beautiful what swift exorcism lies in this course of proceeding, and how at the first real glimpse of it all foul spirits and sickly torments prepare to vanish.

"I hope you will not often have experience of this, poor child. And don't object that your duties are so insignificant; they are to be reckoned of infinite significance and alone important to you. Were it but the more perfect regulation of your apartments, the sorting-away of your clothes and trinkets, the arranging of your papers—'Whatsoever thy hand findeth to do, *do it* with all thy might,' and all thy worth and constancy. Much more, if your duties are of evidently higher, wider scope; if you have brothers, sisters, a father, a mother, weigh earnestly what claim does lie upon you, on behalf of each, and consider it as the one thing needful, to pay *them* more and more honestly and nobly what you owe. What matter how miserable one is, if one can do that? That is the sure and steady disconnection and extinction of whatsoever miseries one has in this world. Other spiritual medicine I never do discover; neither, I believe, does other exist, or need to exist.

"For the rest, dear child, you are evidently too severe upon yourself; these bad thoughts don't make you a 'wicked girl,' not until you yield to them; the excess of your remorse and self-abhorrence is itself proof of some height of nobleness in you. We have all of us to be taught by *stripes*, by sufferings—won't learn otherwise. Courage, courage! As to fasting, penance, etc., that is all become a ghastly matter; have nothing to do with that; *work, work*, and be careful about nothing else. Choose with your utmost skill among your companions and coevals some real associates; be not too much alone with your thoughts, which are by nature bottomless. Finally, be careful of your health; bodily ill-health, unknown to your inexperience, may have much to do with the miseries. Farewell.          T. CARLYLE."

## 37.

RALPH WALDO EMERSON TO ALEXANDER IRELAND.

"LIVERPOOL, *August* 30, 1833.

"MY DEAR SIR,—A shower of rain, which hinders my visiting, gives me an opportunity of fulfilling my promise to send you an account of my visit to Mr. Carlyle and to Mr. Wordsworth. I was fortunate enough to find both of them at home. Mr. C. lives among some desolate hills in the parish of Dunscore, fifteen or sixteen miles from Dumfries. He had heard of my purpose from his friend who gave me my letter, and insisted on dismissing my gig, which went back to Dumfries to return for me the next day in time to secure my seat in the evening coach for the South. So I spent near twenty-four hours with him. He lives with his wife, a most agreeable and accomplished woman, in perfect solitude. There is not a person to speak to within seven miles. He is the most simple, frank, amiable person. I became acquainted with him at once; we walked over several miles of hills and talked upon all the great questions which interest us most. The comfort of meeting a man of genius is that he speaks sincerely, that he feels himself to be so rich that he is above the meanness of pretending to knowledge which he has not; and Carlyle does not pretend to have solved the great problems, but rather to be an observer of their solution as it goes forward in the world. I asked him at what religious development the concluding passage in his piece in the *Edinburgh Review* upon German literature (say five years ago), and some passages in the piece called ' Characteristics,' pointed. He replied that he was not competent to state it even to himself; he wanted rather to see. My own feeling was that I had met with men of far less power who had yet greater insight into religious truth. He is, as you might guess from his papers, the most catholic of philosophers; he forgives and loves everybody, and wishes each to struggle on in his own place and arrive at his own ends. But his respect for eminent men, or rather his scale of eminence, is rather the reverse of the popular scale. Scott, Mackintosh, Jeffrey, Gibbon—even Bacon— are no heroes of his. Stranger yet, he hardly admires Socrates, the glory of the Greek world; but Burns and Samuel Johnson. Mirabeau, he said, interested him; and I suppose whoever else has given himself with all his heart to a leading instinct, and has not *calculated* too much. But I cannot think of sketching even his opinions, or repeating his conversation here. I will cheerfully do it when you visit me in America. He talks finely, seems to love the broad Scotch, and I loved him very much at once. I am afraid he finds his entire solitude tedious; but I could not help congratulating him upon his treasure in his wife, and I hope they will not leave the moors, 'tis so much better for a man of letters to nurse himself in seclusion than to be filed down to the common level by the compliances and imitations of city society.

"The third day afterwards I called upon Mr. Wordsworth at Rydal Mount. He received me with much kindness, and remembered up all his American acquaintance. He had very much to say about the evils of superficial education, both in this country and in mine. He thinks the intellectual tuition of society is going on out of all proportion faster than its moral training, which last is essential to all education. He doesn't wish to hear of schools of tuition; it is the education of circumstances which he values, and much more to this point. He says that he is not in haste to publish more poetry, for many reasons; but that what he has written will at some time be given to the world. He led me out into a walk in his grounds, where, he said, màny thousands of his lines were composed, and repeated to me those beautiful sonnets which he has just finished, upon the occasion of his recent visit to Fingal's Cave at Staffa. I hope he will print them speedily. The third is a gem. He was so benevolently anxious to impress upon me my social duties as an American citizen that he accompanied me near a mile from his house, talking vehemently, and ever and anon stopping short to imprint his words. I noted down some of his words when I got home, and you may see them in Boston, Massachusetts, when you will. I enjoyed both my visits highly, and shall always esteem your Britain very highly in love for its wise and good men's sake. I remember with much pleasure my visit to Edinburgh, and my short acquaintance with yourself. It will give me great pleasure to hear from you—to know your thoughts. Every man that was ever born has some that are peculiar. Present my respects to your father and family. Your friend and servant,

"R. WALDO EMERSON."

# PART IV

LETTERS ADDRESSED TO

MRS. BASIL MONTAGU AND B. W. PROCTER

BY

MR. THOMAS CARLYLE

# LETTERS OF THOMAS CARLYLE

ADDRESSED TO

## Mrs. BASIL MONTAGU and B. W. PROCTER.

---

"MAINHILL, ECCLEFECHAN, 20*th May*, 1825.

"MY DEAR MADAM,—I were inexcusable had this long silence been wilful: the kind and delightful letter which you sent me merited at least a prompt and thankful answer. Your generous anxieties for my welfare should not have been met by months of total silence. My apology is a trite but yet a faithful one. Your letter reached me, after various retardations, in a scene of petty business and petty engagement; and I had no choice but either to write inanities in reply to elegant and friendly sense, or to wait with patience for a calmer day.

"That calmer day has not yet come. Ever since I left you I have been so shifted and shovelled to and fro among men and things of the most discordant character that my thoughts have altogether lost their regular arrangement. The small citadel of my intellectual identity has almost yielded to so many inroads; at least the garrison, weary of never-ending battle and imperfect conquest, have now locked the gates, and scarcely ever sally out at all. I live without thinking or theorizing, as the passing hour directs; and any true expression of *myself* in writing, or even speech, is a problem of unusual difficulty. You see my situation: I have been disturbed and dissipated till I have become exhausted and stupid. Yesterday I was buying chairs and curtains, and even crockery, and there is still no rest till three weeks after Whitsunday! Add to all this that three days ago, in cutting sticks for certain rows of peas which I am cultivating here, I tore my thumb, so that it winces every line I write! But can the Ethiopian change his skin, or the dolt his dulness, by confession and complaint? I had much rather you should think me stupid than ungrateful; so I write *to-day* without further explanation or apology, which would but aggravate the evil either way. When I think of all your conduct towards me, I confess I am forced to pronounce it *magnanimous*. From the first, you had faith enough in human nature to believe that under the vinegar surface of an atrabiliar character there might lurk some touch of principle and affection; notwithstanding my repulsive aspect, you followed me with unwearied kindness, while near you;

and now that I am far off, and you suspect me of stealing from you the spirit of your most valued friend, you still think tenderly of me; you send me cheering words into my solitude. Amid these rude moors a little dove-like messenger arrives to tell me that I am not forgotten, that I still live in the memories and wishes of some noble souls. Believe me, I am not unthankful for this ; I am poor in heart, but not entirely a bankrupt. There are moments when the thought of these things makes me ten years younger, when I feel with what fervid gratitude I should have welcomed sympathy, or the very show of sympathy, from such a quarter, had it then been offered me; and vow that *yet*, changed as matters are, you shall not escape me, that I *will* yet understand you and love you, and be understood and loved by you. I did you injustice; I never *saw* you till about to lose you. Base Judean that I was! Can you forgive without forgetting me? I hope yet to be near you long and often, and to taste in your society the purest pleasure, that of fellow-feeling with a generous and cultivated mind. How rare it is in life, and what were life without it! Forgive me if you can. If my affection and gratitude have any value in your eyes, you are like to be no loser by my error. I felt it before I left you; I feel it still more deeply now.

"I must also entreat you to free me from the charge

of alienating Mr. Irving from the friend whom he should value most. I have no such influence as you ascribe to me; and if I had, I hope I should be sorry so to use it. Edward Irving must be blind indeed if he does not see that you love him with the affection of a mother; and he were no longer *my* Edward if this itself did not bind him to you. Depend on it, my dear madam, for *this* time you are wrong. Our friend does not love you or esteem you less: it is only his multifarious purposes and ever-shifting avocations that change the outward aspect of his conduct. He was my earliest, almost my only friend, and yet for two years after he began to reign among you, I could not wring a single letter from him! You must tolerate such things in him, and still be kind to him, and not forsake him; in his present circumstances, however it may fare with him, your counsel might be doubly precious. For Mrs. —— also I must say a friendly word. She does not hate you; she respects you, and desires your friendship. Will you believe that I had actually engaged to be her mediator with you, and to bring about an intimacy which I saw might be so profitable to her! On a narrower inspection, I renounced the project in despair; yet I feel convinced you would like her, were she fully known to you. That you disagreed at first cannot be strange to me; her primary impression of you was in some degree like my own, and you had not the toleration for her inexperience which you had for mine. I confess I have still some hope from the flight of years; where one sees a want and the means of supplying it, one would gladly bring about a combination. Had you been Mrs. ——'s sister, she had never been a mystic devotee, and never trod the thorny paths through which her vehement, sincere, and misdirected spirit is struggling after what, in all its forms, is the highest aim of mortals—Moral Truth. But the [letter torn] judgment of character must be fallible in your eyes! [torn] will go for nothing.

"But ill-success in this attempt does not deter me from a new one. You know Miss Welsh of Haddington, if not in name, at least in character and from her friends. I was with her at her mother's when you wrote to me. Jane knew the writer by the portraiture of *two* not unfriendly friends, admired and liked the letter, and begged of me to let her keep it.

"She had refused an invitation to Pentonville: one of her chief regrets in declining it was the veto put on her commencing an acquaintance with you.

"She asked would you not write to *her*. I engaged to try, and now will you? Can you?

"This young lady is a person whom you will love and tend as a daughter when you meet; an ardent, generous, gifted being, banished to the pettinesses of a country town; loving, adoring the excellent in all its phases, but without models, advisers, or sympathy. Six years ago she lost her father, the only person who had ever understood her: since that hour she has never mentioned his name; she never alludes to him yet without an agony of tears.

"It was Mr. Irving's wish, and mine, and, most of all, her own, to have you for her friend; that she should live beside you till she understood you; that she might have at least one model to study, one woman with a mind as warm and rich to show her by living example how the most complex destiny might be wisely managed. Separated by space, could you draw near to one another by the imperfect medium of letters? Jane thinks it would abate the 'awe' which she must necessarily feel on first meeting with you personally. She wishes it; I also if it were attainable: is it not?

"I should now depict my doings and my circumstances, my farming and my gardening, literature and dietetics. All this demands another sheet, which I trust you will *very* soon afford me opportunity of sending. I am getting healthier and happier, living by the strictest letter of the Badamian Code, and hoping steadfastly to conquer the baleful monster which has crushed me to the dust so long. Do write as soon as possible; and do *not* pay the postage.

"I am unjust to you no more, but ever most sincerely yours, THOMAS CARLYLE."

" You will make my best respects to Mr. Montagu, and to Mrs. and Mr. Procter. The latter, I hope, will by-and-by bethink him of his promise, and let me have a sheet of literary news.

" Is my dear Badams with you? Did you get the book I sent for him? Excuse this miserable letter. I am sick and in confusion. Next time I will do better."

---

TO MRS. MONTAGU, 25 BEDFORD SQUARE, LONDON.

"21 COMLEY BANK, 25th December, 1826.

"MY DEAR MADAM,—At length my most nervous bookseller has determined, even in these 'worst of times,' as he calls them, on sending forth his literary cargo; an heroic resolution, which he has not adopted till after the most painful consultation, and after calculating as if by astrological science the propitious day and minute indicated by the horoscope of the work. I know not whether it is right to laugh at this poor profit-and-loss philosopher in his pitiable quandary; for his one true God being Mammon, he does worship him with an edifying devoutness; but, at all events, I may rejoice that this favorable conjunction of the stars has at length actually occurred, which after four months' imprisonment in Ballantyne's warehouses now takes this feeble concern finally off my hands, and enables me, among many other important duties, to discharge not the least important one—that of paying my debt to you.

"I have really owed you long, but you are a patient creditor, and know too, I am persuaded, that though letters are the symbol of attention and regard, the thing signified may often exist in full strength without the sign. Indeed, indeed, my dear madam, I am not mad enough to forget you: the more I see of the world and myself the less tendency have I that way, the more do I feel that in this my wilderness journey I have found but *one* Mrs. Montagu, and that, except in virtue of peculiar good-fortune, I had no right to calculate on even finding one. A hundred times do I regret that you are not here, or I there: but I say to myself, we shall surely meet again on this side the wall of Night; and you will find me wiser, and I shall know you better, and love and reverence you more. Meantime, as conscience whispers, what are protestations? Nothing, or worse than nothing: therefore let us leave them.

"Of my late history I need not speak, for you already know it: I am wedded; to the best of wives, and with all the elements of enjoyment richly ministered to me, and health—rather worse than even it was wont to be. Sad contradiction! But I were no apt scholar if I had not learned long ago, with my friend Tieck, that 'in the fairest sunshine a shadow chases us; that in the softest music there is a tone which chides.'

"I sometimes hope that I shall be well: at other

times I determine to be *wise* in spite of sickness, and feel that wisdom is better even than health; and I dismiss the lying cozener Hope entirely, and fancy I perceive that even the rocky land of Sorrow is not without a heavenly radiance overspreading it, lovelier than aught that this Earth, with all its joys, can give us. At all events, what right have we to murmur? It is the common lot: the Persian King could not find three happy men in the wide world to write the names of on his queen's tomb, or the Philosopher would have recalled her from death. Every son of Adam has his task to toil at, and his stripes to bear for doing it wrong. There is one deadly error we commit at our entrance on life, and sooner or later we must lay it aside, for till then there is neither peace nor rest for us in this world: we all start, I have observed, with the tacit persuasion that whatever become of others, we (the illustrious all-important *we*) are entitled of *right* to be *entirely fortunate*, to accumulate all knowledge, beauty, health, and earthly felicity in *our* sacred person, and so pass *our* most sovereign days in rosy bowers, with Distress never seen by us, except as an interesting shade in the distance of our landscape. Alas! what comes of it? Providence will not treat us thus—nay, with reverence be it spoken, cannot treat us thus; and so we fight and fret against His laws, and cease not from our mad, harassing delusion till Experience have beaten it out of us with many chastisements.

"Most, indeed, never fully unlearn it all their days, but continue to the last to believe that in their lot in life they are *unjustly* treated, and cease not from foolish hopes, and still stand in new amazement that they should be disappointed — so very strangely, so *unfairly!* This class is certainly the most pitiable of all, for an Action of Damages against Providence is surely no promising lawsuit.

"But I must descend from Life in general to Life in Edinburgh. In spite of ill-health, I reckon myself moderately happy here, much happier than men usually are, or than such a fool as I deserves to be. My good wife exceeds all my hopes, and is in truth, I believe, among the best women that the world contains. The philosophy of the heart is far better than that of the understanding. She loves me with her whole soul, and this one sentiment has taught her much that I have long been vainly at the Schools to learn. Good Jane! She is sitting by me knitting you a purse: you must not cease to love her, for she deserves it, and few love you better. Of society, in this modern Athens, we have no want, but rather a superabundance, which, however, we are fast and successfully reducing down to the fit measure. True it is, one meets with many a Turk in grain among these people; but it is some comfort to know beforehand that Turks are, have been, and forever will be; and to understand that from a Turk no Christian word or deed can rationally be expected. Let the people speak in the Turkish dialect, in Heaven's name! It is their own, and they have no other. A better class of persons, too, are to be found here and there; a sober, discreet, logic-loving, moderately well-informed class: with these I talk and enjoy myself; but only talk as from an upper window to people on the street; into the house (of my spirit) I cannot admit them; and the unwise wonderment they exhibit when I do but show them the lobby warns me to lose no time in again slamming to the door. But what of society? Round our own hearth is society enough, with a blessing. I read books, or like the Roman poet and so many British ones, 'disport on paper;' and many a still evening when I stand in our little flower-garden (it is fully larger than two bedquilts), and smoke my pipe in peace, and look at the reflection of the distant city lamps, and hear the faint murmur of its tumult, I feel no little pleasure in the thought of 'my own four walls,' and what they hold.

"On the whole, what I chiefly want is occupation; which when 'the times grow better,' or my own 'genius' gets more alert and thorough-going, will not fail, I suppose, to present itself. Idle I am not altogether, yet not occupied as I should be; for to dig in the mines of Plutus, and sell the gift of God (and such is every man's small fraction of intellectual talent) for a piece of money is a measure I am not inclined to; and for *invention*, for Art of any sort, I feel myself too helpless and undetermined. Some day—oh that the day were here!—I shall surely speak out these things that are lying in me, and giving me no sleep till they are spoken! Or else if the Fates would be so kind as show me—that I had nothing to say! This, perhaps, is the real secret of it, after all; a hard result, yet not intolerable, were it once clear and certain. Literature, it seems, is to be my trade; but the present aspects of it among us seem to me peculiarly perplexed and uninviting. I love it not: in fact, I have almost quitted modern reading: lower down than the Restoration I rarely venture in English. These men, these Hookers, Bacons, Brownes, were *men;* but for our present 'men of letters,' our dandy wits, our utilitarian philosophers, our novel, play, sonnet, and song manufacturers, I shall only say, May the Lord pity us and them! But enough of this! For what am I that I should censure? Less than the least in Israel.

"It is time that I devote a word or two to others, having spent the whole sheet on myself. You say nothing of your health: am I to consider you as recovered? I dare scarcely believe it: yet perhaps you *are* recovering. Alas! sorrow has long been familiar to you; and ill-health is but one of the many forms under which it too frequently pursues such beings from the cradle to the grave. But the heart, too, according to the old similitude, is sometimes like a spicy flower, which yields not its sweetest perfume till it be *crushed*. Of Charles's history at Cambridge I am sorry to hear, though it does not surprise me much, or in any wise diminish my faith in his character and capabilities. It shows only that, venerating Science, and this alone, he has formed too lofty an estimate of its Expositors and Institutions: he looked for Sages, such as are not to be found on this clay planet; he meets with Drivellers, and his heart is too proud to yield their gowns and maces what it denies their minds. He is far too proud, poor fellow; and that is a failing which he must and will lay aside. But what is to be done with him for the present? At Cambridge, in his present mood, he must not continue; in Edinburgh I durst not predict his fate: he might find the right road, or deviate farther from it than ever. Again and again I say, if I can be of *any* service, command me. And in the meanwhile fear not for your stormful, headstrong, high-minded boy. There is metal in him which no fire can utterly consume, and one way or other (with more or less suffering to himself, but with certainty, as I believe), it will be fused and purified, and the wayward youth will be a wise and generous man.

"I have finished my sheet, and more I must deny myself at present. Will you get these tomes conveyed to Badams, my own good Badams, whom I swear I had rather see than any ten men in England? I have begged of him to write, but I know he will not: my good wishes are always with him. From you I expect better things, being minded to become a better correspondent myself. Will you make my kindest compliments to Mr. Montagu, and all your household, and believe me ever, my dear madam,

"Your affectionate friend,

"T. CARLYLE."

TO B. W. PROCTER, ESQ., 25 BEDFORD SQUARE, LONDON.

"EDINBURGH, 21 COMLEY BANK, 17th January, 1828.

"MY DEAR SIR,—I have long felt that I owed you a letter of the kindest thanks: yet now I am not intending to repay you, but rather to increase my debt by a new request of favors. The case is this: I am, since yesterday, a candidate for the Moral Philosophy Professorship in the University of St. Andrews, soon to be vacated by the transferrence of Dr. Chalmers to Edinburgh; and thus my task for the present is to dun all such of my friends as have a literary reputation for Testimonials in my behalf. Considerable support in this way I can promise myself, and, except in this way, I have no hope of any;

being altogether unconnected, as you know, either with Church or State, and, at all events, unfit for the dark ways of political intrigue, which too often, I am sorry to own, lead safeliest and soonest to such a goal as I am now aiming at. However, the St. Andrews Professors, the electors to this office, boast much that they have amended their ways; and, under terror of the late Royal Commission, who knows but the Melville interest *may* have ceased to be omnipotent there. In this case I have some hope, in any other case little; but in all cases happily no great degree of fear. Meanwhile the business is to try, and try with my whole might, since I have entered on the enterprise. Your friend Mr. Jeffrey is my Palinurus, and forwards me with great heartiness: I may also reckon on the warm support of Wilson, Leslie, Brewster, and other men of mark in this city; and now I am writing to London for yours and Mr. Montagu's. If you and he, or you yourself, can with freedom speak any word in my favor, I cannot doubt that you will do it readily.

"Perhaps you will tell me that you have no special judgment in matters philosophic, and think within yourself that any skill *I* may have possessed in this province must have been kept with extreme secrecy, during our acquaintance, in the recesses of my own consciousness. It were now too late to prove the error of these opinions, especially *the lat-*

*ter;* but I may observe, in refutation, that it is not
skill in Philosophy alone, but general talent, and *all*
sorts of literary gifts that come into play here; in
which case, who is better entitled to speak than
'Barry Cornwall,' if so be his conscience will let
him? The Editor of Bacon will be another name of
weight in a professional election: may I count on
your laying this matter before him, and Mrs. Montagu's friendly intervention in inciting him to act?
I would have written to him in particular; but why,
thought I, *two* letters on one subject, and to one
house? The rather that I am busy to a degree;
for though the business may not be settled for many
months, it is judged important by my friends that I
should produce my documents without delay. Shall
I hope, then, to ornament my little list with two
other names? To see you, an English Poet, beside
a Scottish one and a German, for Goethe also is
written to? I believe I shall. For the rest, I need
give you no directions as to the *form* of your Testi-
monial; this being altogether arbitrary, equally effectual were it a Letter to me, or a Letter to the
Principal and Professors of St. Andrews, or a general
*Testamur* directed to all men at large. Edward Irving, moreover, knows the whole matter, and can explain it all if you have any difficulty, which, however,
you will not have. And now enough of this poor
business! only do not think me a *sorner* on your

friendliness, and I will say no more about the matter. Speak for me also to Mr. Montagu, and explain to him why I have not spoken for myself. Do I not hereby give you a full *power of attorney;* and for which you are to be paid—in wind-money, on the other side of the Border!

"What do I not owe you already for one of the kindest and most pleasant friends I ever had! Francis Jeffrey is a man meant by Nature to be an intellectual Ariel, with a light etherealness of spirit which the weight of whole Courts of Session resting on it for quarter-centuries has not been able utterly to suppress. There is a glance in the eyes of the man which almost prompts you to take him in your arms. Alas that Mammon should be able to hire such servants, even though they continue to despise him!

"And where are you, my Friend? What is become of your seven-stringed shell that once gave such notes of melody? Do you not reckon it a sin and a shame to bury that fine sense, that truly Artist-spirit, under a load of week-day business? Ought not your light to shine before men, in this season of dim eclipse, when the opaque genius of Utility is shedding disastrous twilight over half the nations? I swear that I will never forgive you, if you keep silence long. My only ground of patience is that you are *lente festinans;* fusing richer ores in the hidden furnace, that they may be cast in fairer moulds of purer metal, and become shapes that will endure forever. Positively this is no idle talk, but the true wish and feeling of my heart, growing clearer to me and clearer the longer I know you. Remember my warning: it is your better genius that speaks through me.

"Do you ever see Mr. Fraser? and why lingers his *Review?* The other day I met a little man, whose eyes sparkled with fire in speaking of it, and he wished to enlist me into his own corps on the other side: I answered that, like Dugald Dalgetty, I had taken bounty under the opposite flag, and so as a true *soldado* could not leave my colors; under which, however, I reckoned myself bound to fight not him, or Gillies, or Cochrane, but the Devil (of Stupidity), and the Devil only. Seeing matters take this turn, the little man's eye grew soft, and he left me.

"What is this periodical of Leigh Hunt's? and have you seen that wondrous Life of Byron? Was it not a thousand pities Hunt had borrowed money of the man he was to disinhume and behead in the course of duty afterwards? But for love or money I cannot see Hunt's book, or anything but extracts of it, and so must hold my tongue. Poor Hunt! He has a strain of music in him too, but poverty and vanity have smote too rudely over the strings. To-day, too, I saw De Quincey: alas, poor Yorick! But enough of gossip also, in which I delight more than I can own in writing. My wife sends her kind regards to you, and I believe would prize two stanzas of your making at no ordinary rate. Is Mrs. Procter well and *safe?* Alas! it was, for all the world, such a night when I sat with you in Russell Street till the ghost-hour, and forgot that Time had shoes of felt. These times and places are all—away. Will Mrs. Montagu accept my thanks at this late date for her so kind and graceful letter? Jane would have written, but was making silk pelisses and cloth pelisses, and had sempstresses, white and black, and only three days ago obtained entire dominion over Frost, and marched the needle-women *out.*

"Adieu. I am ever yours,

"T. CARLYLE."

---

TO MRS. MONTAGU, 25 BEDFORD SQUARE, LONDON.

"CRAIGENPUTTOCH, DUMFRIES, 13*th November,* 1829.

"MY DEAR MADAM,—After a long silence, or mere listening with indirect replies, I again address you, and on the humblest possible subject: a matter of business, relating entirely to myself. Why I trouble *you* in such a case, your helpfulness in past times and constant readiness to do me service will sufficiently explain. At the end of your last letter there occurs a little incidental notice of some opening for a medical man in Warwick, coupled with an advice from Badams that it might be worth my brother's attention. Now it so chances that to my brother, at this season, this announcement is of all others the most interesting. The worthy Doctor has crammed himself with all manner of Scottish, English, and Continental Science in this department; and, ever since his return, has been straining his eyes to discover some spot where he might turn it to some account for himself and others; manifesting in the meanwhile not a little impatience that no such spot was to be found, but that Fate should inthrall free Physic, and condemn so bright a candle to burn altogether under a bushel. On our return from Edinburgh I transmitted him your tidings, on which he wrote instantly to Badams for further information; wrote also to me that he thought the outlook highly promising; and, in fine, this night, has ridden up hither, some five-and-thirty miles (from Scotsbrig) to take counsel with me on the subject, and lament that Badams has given him no answer. My petition, therefore, is that *you* would have the goodness to help the honest adventurer in this affair, and procure for him, by such ways as lie open to you, what light can be had in regard to the actual, practical aspect it presents. My own opinion is that a very little encouragement would bring the man to Warwick, for he is fond of England, and utterly wearied of idleness, as *passiveness* at his age may with little injustice be named. My devout prayer, too, has long been that he were settled somewhere, with any rational prospect; for he has a real solidity, both of talent and character, as I judge, and wants nothing but Action to make him a very sufficient fellow. Do, pray, therefore, help the embryo Hippocrates a little, if you can! He will wait here some eight days, in expectation of your writing, and perhaps also persuading Badams to write: nay, at any time I can forward the news to him into Annandale within a week of their arrival. Write what you know without apprehension of consequences: honest Jack risks little by any such adventure, *having* little save a clear head and a stout honest heart, which are not so easily lost and won. For my own share, I, too, am getting fond of Warwick: it is in the heart of *Old* England, whither I should then have a pretext for coming; nay, it is within a day's journey of London, where, among other wondrous things, there is ' a 25 Bedford Square.'

"You are not to account this a Letter, but only a sort of commercial Message, a Man-of-Business Commission. 'Do you know, Mr. ——,' said John Wilson once, in my hearing, to a noted writer to the Signet, proud enough of his Signet honors, 'there is nothing in nature that I detest so much as a Man of Business.' He of the Signet had imagined himself high in the other's good graces, and now of a sudden saw himself quite stranded, and left alone on the beach.

"I am thinking to take the Correspondence with you out of my wife's hands, so languidly does she manage it; and of old times it was altogether *mine*. I know not that I have yet found, or shall ever find, any correspondent to replace you.

"You will kindly remember me to Mr. Procter and his lady, in whose welfare I must always feel a friend's interest. This is not altogether 'words,' and yet what more can I make it?

"Assure Mr. Montagu that his book was the most delightful I have read for many days. Your hand also was often visible in it. Why does he not publish more such? I have got old Ascham, and read a little of him, when I have done work, every evening. Do you ever see Edward Irving? He stretched himself out here on the moors, under the free sky, for one day beside me, and was the *same* honest soul as of old. Badams will not write to me, I know, but some day I will see him and make him speak.

"Believe me ever, my dear madam,
       "Your affectionate friend,
              "THOMAS CARLYLE."

TO MRS. MONTAGU, 25 BEDFORD SQUARE, LONDON.

"CRAIGENPUTTOCH, 27th October, 1830.

"MY DEAR FRIEND,—While I wait in the confident though somewhat unaccountably deferred anticipation of a kind answer from you to a kind message, come tidings to my wife that such message is still only looked for 'through the portal of Hope;' in plain prose, that my last letter has lost its way, did not reach, and now never will reach, you! This is the more singular, as the like never happened in my past experience, and now, as indeed misfortune usually does, comes doubly. Much about the time when I wrote your letter, I despatched another to Weimar: and here on the same Wednesday night arrive, side by side, two announcements, from you and from Goethe, that both letters have miscarried! Goethe's I have satisfactorily traced to the post-office, and hope there may have been some oblivion on the part of my venerable correspondent; neither is this, though less likely, in your case, a quite impossible supposition. At all events, true it is that, some two months ago I did actually write you a most densely filled letter, one which if it did me any justice must have been filled, moreover, with the friendliest sentiments. I can still recollect of it that I entreated earnestly you would never forget me, would from time to time send me notice of your good or evil

11*

fortune, though I myself (for lack of historical incident in these solitudes) were silent, assuring you, of
what is still true, that *I* was nowise of the forgetting
species, but blessed or burdened with one of your
perennial memories, and a hard and stony heart,
whereon truly only *diamonds* would write; but the
Love-charm and Think-of-me once written stood in-
effaceable, defying all time and weather. Such statement, whereof I could make an affidavit were it
needful, will be a light for you to explain several
things; above all, will absolve from the crime of in-
difference and negligence, which crime towards you,
at least, it will be forever impossible for me to fall
into. Believe this, for it is morally and even phys-
iologically true.

"We hear with real sorrow of the domestic mis-
chances that come upon you; from which, in this
world, no wisdom will secure us.

"Happily the consciousness you mention is a bul-
wark which keeps our inward citadel, or proper Self,
unharmed, unimpregnable, whatever havoc there
may be in the outworks. Let us study to maintain
this, and let those others go their way, which, indeed,
is natural for them. When I think of the miserable
A. and of many like him, I could feel as if our old
fathers who believed in witchcraft and Possession
were nearer the truth than we.

"It is strange how vice, like a poisonous ingredient

thrown into some fermenting mixture, will, in small beginnings, seize on the young heart, and proceed there, tainting, enlarging, till the whole soul, and all the universe it holds, is blackened, blasted, rent asunder with it, and the man that walked in the midst of us is clutched, as it were, by some unseen devil, and hurled into abysses of Despair and Madness, which lie closer than we think on the path of every one. Let us hope (for this is the Place of Hope) that for himself reformation is still possible; that, at least and worst, to the friends that cannot save him, his future misdoings will be harmless.

"Poor Hazlitt! He, too, is one of the victims to the Moloch Spirit of this Time—a Time when Selfishness and Baseness, dizened out with rouge and a little theatrical frippery, has fearlessly seated herself on high places, and preaches forth her Creed of Profit and Loss as the last Gospel for men; when the thing that calls itself God's Church is a den of Unclean Beasts, from which the honest-hearted turns away with loathing; when, between the Utilitarians and the Millenarians, and the dense dust and vapor they have raised up, the Temple of the Universe has become to the most invisible; and the devout spirit that will not blind itself cannot worship, and knows not what or how to worship, and so wanders in aimless pilgrimages, and lives without God in the world! In Hazlitt, as in Byron and Burns and so many others in their degree, there lay some tone of the 'eternal melodies,' which he could not fashion into terrestrial music, but which uttered itself only in harsh jarrings and inarticulate cries of pain.  Poor Hazlitt!  There is one star less in the heavens, though a twinkling, dimmed one; while the street-lamps and horn lanterns are all burning, with their whale-oil or coal gas, as before!  These the street passenger and drayman and bearer of burden will prize and bless; but in the lonely journeys and far voyages (of Thought) the traveller will miss the other.

" I should give you some glimpse into our way of life here, but know not how in such compass to do it.  A strange contrast it must be to yours.  If London is the noisiest, busiest spot on the earth, this is about the stillest and most solitary.  The road hither *ends* at our house : to see a lime-cart or market-cart struggling along the broken moor, till it reach gravel and wheel-ruts, and scent the Dominion of Commerce from afar, is an incident which, especially in winter, we almost mark in our journals.  In this meek, pale sunshine of October, in this grave-like silence, there is something ghostly; were it not that our meadows are of peat-bog and not of asphodel, and our hearts too full of earthly passions and cares, you might fancy it the abode of spirits, not of men and fleecy or hairy cattle.  I have a rough broken path along the neighboring hill-side, two miles in length, where

I take a walk (sometimes as I would take physic)
and see over Ayrshire and Galloway, far and wide,
nothing but granite mountains and idle moors; save
that here and there the cottage trees and smoke, with
its patch of cornfield painfully won from the desert,
indicate that man's two hands are there, who, like the
cony, has built himself a nest in the rocks. On the
whole, an original scene for studying in. Private as
heart could wish; and possessing in this one thought,
that it positively *is* a scene, and dates since the day
when Eternity became Time, and was created by
God—the source, could one but draw from it, of
innumerable, inexhaustible others. Here, truly, is
the place for thinking, if you have any faculty that
way. Since I came hither I have seen into various
things. In my wife, too, I have the clearest, most
Scotch-logical, yet the eagerest Disciple and Convert.
For the rest, I read and write and smoke assiduously,
as I was wont: one day I hope to give you one of
the most surprising *books* you have met with lately.
Am I happy? My theory was and is that the man
who cannot be happy (as happy as is needful) where-
soever God's sky overspans him, and men forbear to
beat him with bludgeons, deserves to be, and will
always be, what one calls miserable. Nevertheless,
we are coming to London, so soon as the yet clearly
audible prohibition of Destiny is withdrawn. Will
it be this winter? Full glad were I too think so;

but there are sad shakings of the head. We had the Jeffreys lately ; *the* Jeffrey a more interesting and better man, a sadder and a wiser, than I had ever seen him. That he missed *you* was no oversight on his part, but ignorance that it would not be an intrusion.

" He looked to Mr. Procter, and Mr. Procter spake not. The like will not occur a second time. Such a visit here, of which we rejoice in one or two perhaps yearly, is a true ' Illumination with the finest Transparencies:' next night, indeed, comes our own still candle, and the past splendor is gone like a dream, but not the memory of it, nor the hope of its return. With Goethe I am more contented the longer I know him ; hard as adamant towards outer fortune, yet with the spirit of a prophet within, and the softest all-embracing heart.

" He is to me the most venerable man now extant, surely the *only* literary man whom, amid all my respect, my admiration, I can view without a considerable admixture of contempt. He tells me yesterday to write soon, ' for days and weeks are growing more and more precious to him.'

" God keep that day long distant! I must add this other passage for the piece of news it brings. Take it in the original too.

" ' *Ein talentvoller junger Mann und glücklicher Uebersetzer beschäftigt sich mit* BURNS : *ich bin dar-*

*auf sehr verlangend.*' ' A talented young man and successful Translator is busy with BURNS: I am very curious for the issue.' You must thank Mr. Montagu for his book on *laughter*, which I have read with pleasure: the other book (of Extracts) my mother has borrowed, and eagerly begs to keep for a second and a *third* perusal: it is among the best books she ever saw, worthy whole cartloads of their new ware. For *poetry* (not mere rhyme and rant or else elegance), a Scotch reviewer is probably the blindest of created things; but in a Scotch peasant there is sometimes life, and a soul of God's making. My own impression is that Nature is still active, and that we are all alive did we but know it!—God bless you. I am ever yours, T. CARLYLE.

" My brother speaks with warmest gratitude of your and Mr. Montagu's kindness. Such friends in such a course as his are indeed invaluable. I too am doubly your debtor for the maternal charge you take of my poor Doctor, whose posture in that wild chaos often fills me with misgivings. Will Mr. Procter, with his bright kind Lady, who is still strangely present with me, be pleased to know that I think of them ?"

THE END.